The Continuing Legacy of Simone Weil

David Pollard

Hamilton Books

An Imprint of
Rowman & Littlefield
Lanham • Boulder • New York • Toronto • Plymouth, UK

Copyright © 2015 by Hamilton Books
4501 Forbes Boulevard, Suite 200, Lanham, Maryland 20706
Hamilton Books Acquisitions Department (301) 459-3366

Unit A, Whitacre Mews, 26-34 Stannary Street,
London SE11 4AB, United Kingdom

All rights reserved

British Library Cataloguing in Publication Information Available

Library of Congress Control Number: 2015933108
ISBN: 978-0-7618-6574-2 (pbk : alk. paper)—ISBN: 978-0-7618-6575-9 (electronic)

Pour Linley
Elle qui aime Dieu dans son aspect impersonnel

Contents

Acknowledgments vii

1 Overview 1
2 Upbringing and Influences 11
3 Encounter 25
4 Spiritual Theologian 45
5 Politics and the Possible 69
6 The Continuing Legacy 93

Bibliography 119

Index 121

Acknowledgments

I am grateful to a number of people who assisted me in the writing of this book. My contacts in the Weil Society of North America have been invaluable for me, writing, as I have been, in Australia, where Simone Weil's life and work are not well known. I would especially like to thank Prof. Larry Schmidt of Toronto who assisted by reading and critiquing early copies of the manuscript. I have also been assisted by the reading and feedback of Miriam Nicholls, Gregory Gibson, Marie Larkin and Hugh Dillon. My wife Linley did an enormous amount of work in reading, reviewing and correcting the work as well as formatting the manuscript. My thanks to her and to all who were of so much help in bringing the work to a conclusion.

Chapter One

Overview

We are approaching the 75th anniversary of Simone Weil's death. In 1943, still in her thirties, she succumbed to a range of conditions and died in England, not quite alone, but certainly unregarded. Weil's formidable reputation was to develop after her death.

In many ways this frail, passionate and candid writer was the exception to the generality of midcentury thinkers. In viewing Weil's life, we see almost every contradiction that could possibly characterize the life and times of an intellectual trying to live authentically in a world adrift. The twenty years leading up to her death, including the years in which she wrote, were momentous, even monstrous, not only for France, but for Europe as a whole and indeed for most of the rest of the world. They saw the breakup of the fragile peace that concluded the Great War. This was followed by the Great Depression. Related to these two developments was the rise of Fascism and Nazism and the fracturing of democracy in much of Europe. The beginnings of the territorial aggression of Italy, Germany and Japan that would lead to a further global war were opportunities presented by the confluence of these events.

Weil was a philosopher, but she would probably have rejected that description as a single word summation of her life. She was embroiled in all the major movements of the twentieth century. She struggled to think through an adequate expression of her religious experiences and to act on them with authenticity: not just to empathize with outcasts but to try to identify with them. Weil was a woman of great intellectual powers, with a prodigious capacity for work and an intense need to be involved, to be shaping, to be effectual. In the course of her thirty-four years she moved from atheism to belief and arguably, in the eyes of some (though not of herself), to sainthood. The last period of her life was her most prolific and profound. Her final writing coincided with the turning point of the Second World War. Weil articulated all that was at stake in that struggle in that she understood the profound moral questions that the War threw up. These questions included the nature of evil, of which the War itself was a symptom. They also included the radical human freedom which was constitutive of the nature of humanity and which therefore made this evil possible. If anyone had insight into the moral origins and conundrums of war, and the Second World War in particular, it was Simone Weil, especially because she had thought so deeply on the origin and effects of force in the world.

SIMONE WEIL'S FORMATION

Weil was born into a Jewish bourgeois family on February 3, 1909, the child of a physician and an energetic and gifted mother who oversaw her education with constant and meticulous attention to it throughout her childhood. She had a brother, Andre Weil, who was to become a world-renowned mathematician. Weil went to the best schools and graduated at age 22 from the École Normale Superieure with the degree Agrégée de Philosophie, from which she went to teach school in provincial France.[1]

Like many French intellectuals, Weil became an active Marxist, though she never joined the Communist Party. She tried to involve herself deeply in a variety of movements supporting workers' rights and participated in union activities. At the age of twenty-four, during her teaching duties at Le Puy, she participated in the General Strike called to protest against general wage cuts and then took a one year's leave of absence from teaching to work in a Renault factory. Weil described herself at this stage of her life as a pacifist. After a short stint, she left the factory and resumed her teaching. In 1936, doubtless to the horror of her parents, she went to Spain to fight on the side of the Republic, and eventually struggled through her pacifist sympathies. As in the case of many of those who went to Spain to defend "democracy" against the Right, her understanding of the nature of the struggle changed as Weil experienced firsthand the brutality of the Left and was more and more affected by the idea that she was becoming complicit in it.

In all this, Weil's life was following a familiar trajectory: the bourgeois intellectual anxious to identify with the working class in their rejection and suffering and to live her one life in an authentic manner. Many of her contemporaries followed more or less the same path. Her maturing and change was a familiar story. George Orwell had a similar experience. The mix of idealism, concern for the working class, rejection of capitalism, suspicion of the Right, the yearning for solidarity—all these were part of a mix of ideas circulating among European and American young intellectuals in the 1930s. It largely explains the profile of the members of the International Brigade which was drawn to Spain to join in the struggle against the Spanish Nationalists.

TRANSFORMATION

One can understand how the Spanish Civil War drew Weil and others to join in and to shed their pacifist commitments. Members of the International Brigade were profoundly ignorant of the cynicism and coercive tendencies of the Left and particularly of the Communist parties which led the struggle. Communism was still relatively new in 1936 and the mass killings of the 1920s and 30s in the Ukraine and Russia were either not known about or not believed, although Weil was a notable exception. Certainly, it was only the firsthand experience of the brutality and violence of the Left in situations of shared struggle which succeeded in educating this cohort of outsiders. Weil carried out some noncombatant duties but after a few months, returned to France with injuries unrelated to the War.

At this juncture Weil's political philosophy and her humanism began to mature and were transformed into something entirely different. Philosophically, she had been immersed in the classical tradition. She had studied Plato and had an excellent grasp of Greek and a number of modern European languages. Weil had come first in the entrance examination for the École Normale Superieure (Simone de Beauvoir had finished second). Philosophy was her *oeuvre* and writing was to be her vehicle. Her philosophy went hand in hand with a commitment to the politics of the Left. The years following Weil's graduation had been years of attempting to integrate herself in a practical manner into the struggles of the Left in France. It is hardly surprising, then, that she became a prolific writer of Leftist articles, addressing issues of concern to French Socialists in a variety of publications. The dominant moral challenges that moved her lay especially in the region of rights, mostly economic rights, and within that mainly those of the working class. Later, Weil would come to assert that rights, as such, were subordinate to obligations. At this stage, however, working class struggle seemed to involve a kind of intrinsic virtue. Her concern was also the driving force behind much of her mature writing and infused her last major work—*The Need for Roots*—which she wrote shortly before her death. Weil always retained her commitment to the poor, the deprived and the oppressed. This commitment, however, rose above Marxist or Socialist ideology and became a commitment to be engaged in the lives of people. Her commitment to political reform slowly transformed itself into a concern for what we might call moral reform, or at least the moral base that should be the foundation for all politics. Weil's earlier concern for the working class evolved into a view on suffering at a deeper level, what it meant and what it could mean. Her agnosticism also began to shift.

Weil's evolving central preoccupation was how to live one's life in a manner consistent with one's true nature, with empathy for and responsibility to others. This preoccupation was not unique to her. It was what has generally been called in modern Western philosophy, the struggle for authenticity. She was not the first philosopher to attempt to join together the traditional preoccupations of Western philosophy (the person, the cosmos, ethics, consciousness, the soul, logic and so on) with the need to live an authentic life in the flesh. This need arose in the mind of latter day philosophers, especially in the nineteenth and early twentieth centuries, from, among other things, a renewed perspective on death. The emerging view was, given that life was lived in the face of death, how could one live with passion, meaning and even redemptively for others? How could we make our lives count?

Weil was aware of this trend in modern philosophy and ultimately her contribution would be somewhat oblique, but she needs to be seen as part of a continuous development within philosophy that put existence at the center of philosophical enquiry. Weil, too, used a number of existentialist concepts in her later work. The silence of God, the leap of faith, the need to come to terms with death and the unique nature of the person as quite distinct from the crowd, all these reflect the then influential existentialist insights.

Weil inherited these and other insights from her philosophical studies, especially under the esteemed Alain.[2] He encouraged her in the view that philosophy needed to be embedded in actual lived experience. Her work in the Renault and other factories in 1934–5 followed Weil's writing of an important essay *Reflections on the causes of Liberty and Social Oppression* where she gave a comprehensive correction to Marx on his notion of technology as the formative driver in culture and the resultant oppression of the worker. Weil agreed that labor grew out of necessity but that this fate could be countered by a greater degree of ownership by workers of the process in which they were engaged and the product which resulted from it. This view later entered *The Need for Roots* of 1942 when she worked in England for De Gaulle on a series of illustrative papers for postwar France. In the meantime, however, Weil's thinking was moving to an altogether different plane.

THE EMERGENCE OF THE RELIGIOUS

Over the period August 1935 to November 1938, Weil, secular philosopher, religious agnostic and Marxist sympathizer, experienced a number of religious encounters for which she had no rational explanation and which changed the course of her life. In this time, she developed from philosopher to mystical theologian, somewhat in the vein of Pascal, and to the amazement of all who knew her and were familiar with her writings until then.

The notion of unmerited and unsought religious consolation is a well developed theme in Catholic mysticism. It is recorded in a number of celebrated instances, for example in the lives of St Theresa, St John of the Cross and St Ignatius Loyola. The earlier mystics' use of the term "consolation" is somewhat akin to Weil's use of the term "possession" and Weil actually rejected the notion of consolation as a mark of God. In Ignatius' case, the ex-soldier turned traveller-searcher, was journeying in 1522 when, while staying at the village of Manresa on the banks of the River Cardoner, he recorded a sudden, immediate and overwhelming presence or immanence of God. The revelation was entirely experiential and he could never explain it except in a series of metaphors. Whatever happened, Ignatius' life after that was radically different from what had gone before. He said that he learned the interior life of faith by an experience of revelation wholly from outside himself.

The experiences of Weil, improbable as they sound for someone living in a secular age, were similar. The first happened in Portugal in 1936 after she had finished working at the factory.

> It was evening and there was a full moon over the sea. The wives of the fishermen were making a tour in procession, carrying candles and singing ancient hymns of heartrending sadness. There the conviction was suddenly borne in upon me that Christianity is preeminently the religion of slaves, that slaves cannot help belonging to it, and I among others.[3]

The second happened in Assisi where Weil was spending two days and where, alone in the chapel of Santa Maria degli Angeli, she described how she was compelled to sink to her knees and, for the first time in her life, to pray.

The third experience occurred at Solesmes in France where Weil and her mother were attending Holy Week services, apparently for reasons of art rather than religious content. Here she encountered and was completely taken by the metaphysical poet George Herbert's famous "Love" (Love bade me welcome…). "It was during one of these recitations that Christ himself came down and took possession of me."[4]

The sudden movement from the intellectual and rational to the affective and intuitive is a universal characteristic of religious mysticism. It appears in the writings of the mystics mentioned above and may be said to be emblematic of the phenomenon of total religious conversion. This is really the mystery at the heart of Weil's life. Its objective *un*likelihood in her life, of all lives, is the authenticating hallmark which distinguishes her life as one of the most intriguing and illuminating of the twentieth century. It was the turning point in her writings.

Chapter 1
THE RELIGIOUS PHENOMENON OF SIMONE WEIL

If one were choosing a person to be the model for Christian theology in the crisis years of the twentieth century, and most especially in the period of the Second World War, 1939–45, one could hardly come up with a more improbable candidate than Weil. The times were very difficult and contending parties, imbued with differing ideologies, were waging wars of unprecedented barbarity. But with bewildering suddenness, a widely recognized woman whose interests to date had been predominantly concerned with the social agenda of the Left, made a transition to Christian mysticism while retaining her life's commitment to the fusion of thought and action. Her immediate grasp of the core of New Testament spirituality was breathtaking. Doubtless, Weil was assisted in this by her close friendship with Fr. J-M Perrin, a Dominican priest and theologian. But it was the complete absence of Catholic theology in her intellectual formation, (she was not educated a Catholic), which gave her subsequent writings their disconcerting edge.

In a few years, Weil visited and wrote on all the classic themes of Catholic theology. These included the nature of the love of God, grace, sin and forgiveness, prayer as attentiveness, atheism as a stage of faith, the absence and silence of God, good and evil, redemptive suffering and many others. Her Protestant contemporary, Karl Barth, dealt with these same issues at about the same time. Unlike Barth, however, Weil's Pascal-like lightning summations dealt with these weighty issues by assertion only, supported occasionally by argument. The methodology was more attuned to revealing to the reader something he or she intuitively already knew, for example the silence of God was evidence of a divine presence: it was the *absence* of God which was felt, and could only be felt, by those who had God within them. Again, on suffering as redemptive, God was present in the most extreme of evil, the crucifixion of Christ being the example, just as he was present in a wafer of bread in the Eucharist: "God gives himself to men either as powerful or as perfect—it is for them to choose."[5]

When we compare the trajectory of the life of St Ignatius of Loyola, mentioned above, with that of Weil, it is hard to conceive a more interesting countertype. Ignatius, after the Cardoner experience, went on to Paris to study, founded the Jesuits, (which went on to become an important element of the Counter Reformation), published his theological insights in his *Spiritual Exercises* and lived a long life of struggle crowned with success. Our other mystic was a creature of the deracinated twentieth century. She was university trained, a writer on social issues, a sometime farm worker, a temporary factory hand. She taught those on the margins, was active in the trade union movement, tried anarchistic socialism and Marxism and, in all this, sought solidarity with workers and social groups. It was precisely her exclusion that formed Weil's diamond hard character. She wrote as the outsider—which perhaps explains why her reception into the Church happened only at the end of her life. She was in her own way as much the mystic type of the twentieth century (especially of these climactic years 1939–42) as Ignatius was of the sixteenth.

SIMONE WEIL'S LATER LIFE

Weil accompanied her parents to Marseilles in 1940. Working briefly on a local farm she dedicated herself to her theological writings, leaving the manuscripts to be kept safe by Gustave Thibon, the farm's owner. These were edited and published as *Gravity and Grace* after the War. They are the core of her theological writings.

Weil left Marseilles for New York in 1942 with her parents where she continued to write while remaining in contact with the Free French in London. From July to November 1942 she wrote extensively, both theology and tracts for the Free French. Weil had never been physically strong, being subject especially to persistent headaches. By then, however, her health was seriously failing as the effects of tuberculosis gradually overwhelmed her frail body. Nevertheless, Weil's literary output continued and in this last *annus mirabilis* of 1942–3, she produced *The Need for Roots*, a text on the nature of man designed to inform the political economy of post War France. She went to London late in 1942 and within six months was hospitalized with tuberculosis complicated by malnutrition. Weil died on August 24, 1943 unlamented by De Gaulle or any of the others of the Free French who clearly resented this female intellectual formerly of the Left and her opinions on the moral state of France then and in their planned future.

PUBLICATION OF SIMONE WEIL'S WORK

Weil's works were slowly gathered together, edited and published after the War. What struck early readers was that they were replete with quotable quotes, much as Pascal's. Their challenge and succinctness also fascinated post-War readers. For example:

> God's great crime against us is to have created us, is the fact of our existence. And in our existence is our great crime against God. When we forgive God for our existence, he forgives us for existing.[6]

Occasionally, her quotes reflect part of her own life journey, for example the struggle she had in reconciling the almost unbearable sufferings of the world with her experience of a loving God. For Weil, her very existence implies complicity in the affliction of the world causing her such anxiety that the love of God becomes impossible. However:

> I reassure myself by remembering that Christ wept on foreseeing the horrors of the destruction of Jerusalem. I hope he will forgive me my compassion.[7]

Weil was a product of the times in which she lived. Her preoccupations were very much those of the active Paris intellectual of the 1920s and 30s. When we contemplate the scope of Weil's life we are drawn to the maelstrom into which her life was swept and which affected so deeply what she had to say. It was partly this drama which Weil addressed. It was certainly the set of questions thrown up by Depression, poverty, war and national humiliation which provided much of the fuel for her passion and insight. We also need to contemplate the fact that what have become her most important writings were not written for publication: they were written as personal reflections. Moreover, the fact that Weil's life was cut short at the age of thirty-four meant that the door slammed shut when her ideas were in their first mode of expression. We do not know whether, had she lived, she might have revised her work, deepened it or even discarded some of it. We are, in effect, looking at a phenomenon in the first stages of emergence without knowing what the final presentation could have been. Of course, it is precisely this quality which gives Weil's writing its sharpness, its uncompromising edge and its confronting challenge.

This book will conclude that the most assured part of Weil's work is her theology and her recasting of some of the basic insights of Christian faith. Here too she was somewhat the product of her age. Weil's core concern was with authenticity and, especially, making her own life work towards some end. Her conclusion was that authenticity must involve a conscious retreat from what she called the personal towards the impersonal and allowing God to enter the vacated space. It is the set of consequences which followed from that which made her a mystical theologian. The possibility of mystical theology, as we shall see later in this work, is especially a Catholic belief. It is the view that the individual may receive a private revelation of God. It is not a common view in Protestantism because it may detract from the universal revelation contained in the Bible. In the Catholic tradition, by contrast, it sits comfortably alongside the biblical and non biblical traditions which constitute the essence of revelation. One may accept such private revelations or not. Taken together, though, Weil's highly refined and intellectualized restatement of the nature of God, of the individual, of providence, of Christian encounter with the Other, of suffering and death all constitute a new language which engages our own generation even more, perhaps, than her own. The questions which she raised are questions which can never be fully answered but she gave us insight into how to take further steps in understanding and integrating these core existential issues of the possibility of faith.

In this sense Weil was more than a creature of the twentieth century, now past. Her relevance has not diminished although much of what she wrote is now *outré*. Her core insights, and most especially her core mystical insights, remain as disturbing and challenging as they were when she penned them. It is timely now to re-present them to a generation which can benefit enormously from them.

Having looked at an overview of her life and work, we shall, in the rest of this work, look more closely (in chapter two) at her life and discern what the cultural and historical influences were which most affected what she wrote. In chapter three we shall look at the nature of her encounter with the Other and discuss what she concluded about the nature of God and the nature of the person which makes such encounter possible. In chapter four we shall examine the manner in which Weil's view of encounter determined her overall spiritual theology which was the most important and lasting aspect of her life's work. The fifth chapter looks at Weil's political writing, most especially the last great work of her life, *The Need for Roots*, which she wrote in 1942–3 just before she died. The final chapter leads to the conclusion that she is, all things considered, more relevant to this century than to the last. Her greatest contributions may be yet to come.

NOTES

1. The *École Normale Superieure* in Paris trained upper school teachers and university academics for careers in public and university education.
2. Emile-Auguste Chartier (1868–1951)
3. Weil, Simone. *Waiting for God.* (Crawford E *trans.*) New York: Harper and Rowe, 1973 p67
4. Ibid p69
5. Weil, Simone. *Gravity and Grace.* (Crawford E and von der Ruhr M *trans*) London: Routledge Classics, 1999 p91ff
6. Panichas, George. *Simone Weil Reader.* Wakefield: Moyer Bell, 1977 p400
7. Weil, Simone *Waiting* p45

Chapter Two

Upbringing and Influences

ORIGINS: THE PARIS OF THE EARLY TWENTIETH CENTURY

Simone Weil's parents were assimilated and non-religious Jews. Her father was a well-regarded physician. Her mother was the child of a wealthy Austrian family. Weil grew up with a mathematician brother (1906–1998) who was to become famous in the area of the mathematics of number theory. She was fortunate in receiving a liberal upbringing, her parents fully conscious of the genius of both Simone and her brother Andre. She acquired an early grasp of the ethical, refusing, at the age of six, to eat sugar because French soldiers at the Front were denied it. This pattern of emulation of the sufferings of others was to recur at the end of her life.

    The Paris in which Weil spent her early years was a world center of intellectual endeavor, style and ideas. France's idea of itself had been tested by its defeat at the hands of Prussia in the Franco-Prussian War of 1871 and the ferocious Paris Commune which followed it. The loss to the new German Empire of the provinces of Alsace and Lorraine had left a dangerous sense of victimhood in the national consciousness, offset to some extent by France's extension of its own empire to remote parts of Africa and Asia, a distraction fully supported by Berlin. The First World War (1914–18) brought France close to defeat again and it was saved only through the successful assembly of a suite of allies to cooperate in the defeat of Germany. The French sought to reverse the humiliation inflicted upon it in 1871 by taking back the two lost provinces and insisting on a punishing peace by which Germany had to admit responsibility for the war, agree to disarm and meet a reparations bill of 132 billion marks, hundreds of billions of dollars in today's money. The French hoped that Germany could be rendered incapable of threatening France by virtue of its ostensible loss of military capacity and by the advent of a truly functioning democratic constitution. This might have been the case had the Treaty been backed by powers willing to enforce it.

Weil was ten when the Treaty of Versailles was signed. The Paris of that era had a strong force of attraction for displaced intellectuals from all over Europe in the disrupted years following the War. France was a generous country and intellectuals migrated there from throughout Europe and from France's wide empire, eager to experience a culture that was open, liberal, experimental and sophisticated. Paris, the City of Light, attracted and fostered artists, writers, composers, the *avant-garde* and the global fashion industry. Of course, other cities, notably London and New York, were also centers of art and design. But Paris seemed unique in its capacity to combine all the elements which constituted the exciting possibilities opened up by the birth of the modern in the post-War world.

It was the Paris of the Third Republic, a political form which had emerged after France's defeat in the Franco-Prussian War. Unlike in Britain, where democratic parliamentary institutions and an independent judiciary had slowly evolved over centuries, France's experience with both was recent and unstable. There were deep currents in the political life of France, among them a nostalgia for the monarchy, a bitter anti-clericalism, a strong propensity among the Left for disempowering the propertied classes and, through all this, a dangerous lack of respect on all sides for the principle of compromise which makes democracy possible. Nevertheless, the Third Republic was the expression of a democratic constitution framing mass politics and France did have, after 1870, a free press and a modern political culture. Despite this, there was a widespread view among the Right, both before and after the War, that France was decadent and open to subversion by forces which were ultimately countercultural, especially global finance, sexual depravity, atheism, socialism and pacifism. This view was reinforced by the victory of the Bolsheviks in Russia in 1917, which seemed, and not only in France, to usher in a new era of threat from the political Left and its worldwide allies. The decadent/nondecadent divide roughly coincided with the Left-Right divide, always toxic in French politics. It became a coda for a suite of cognate views on how France's future should develop into a more inclusive and just society able to deliver the politics France deserved. The notion of a decadent Third Republic which did not deserve to survive, by virtue of its failings, was to influence Weil and most of her contemporaries, especially as the 1940 occupation of France spelled its end and handed France over to those who had little core respect for either democracy or the principle of compromise which lay at its core.

Weil flourished at that moment in French history, from the mid-1930s to the early 1940s, when the Third Republic was unraveling and the French political leadership embarked on the politically necessary but difficult task of bringing yet another political framework to birth. Her views on and her experience of the Third Republic focused what were to become the political writings of her last years. Her totally French political milieu, though, was to limit Weil's breadth of vision in imagining what France might be, a view we shall examine later.

Following the First World War, and a period of interrupted education as the family followed the father during his period of service, Weil became a regular student at the Laval Lycée and then the Lycée Fenelon. She was formed by a classical education, becoming fluent in Greek and Latin as well as in modern languages. It was during these early years of high school that Weil began to suffer the debilitating headaches which were to recur throughout her life. What precisely these headaches were remains a mystery but her endemic poor health was to make her casual approach to them all the more mysterious.

Weil was never physically robust and was delicate in different ways over the course of her life. This natural predisposition was made worse later on by her regimes of self-denial (fasting, sleeping rough) and self-effacement. It is part of the mystery of Weil that we do not know how much of her ill-health was inherited and how much was the natural consequence of her self-neglect. In any event, she began to suffer and to reflect on her sufferings at about this stage of her life just as she was maturing into the model classical student.

At the age of 16, Weil took the baccalaureate with a specialization in philosophy. On graduating, she went on to study philosophy at the Lycée Henri IV where she remained for three years. In 1928, at the age of 19, she took the entrance examination for the École Normale Superieure and, over the course of her studies, became a much-discussed exponent of Left politics and a supporter and theoretician of the trade union movement.

Weil held ferocious views on the plight and rights of the poor and became an activist for workers' rights. This was not an uncommon stance among the Left Bank intellectuals of the interwar years. France had a long history of Left discourse, going back to the Revolution and much of the pattern of French politics can be seen as a struggle between Left and Right. These destructive struggles were not to be put aside to any significant degree until the proclamation of the Fifth Republic after the Second World War.

Like many of her generation, Weil espoused pacifism while a student. Pacifism was a worldwide movement at the time with strong sets of adherents in parties of the Left. Most of those who designated themselves pacifist in the 1920s dropped their objections to war in principle once the likely effect of the German rearmament of the 1930s became apparent.

Her course at the École Normale Superieure led to a competitive civil service examination enabling Weil to teach in the public system. Her graduation gave her the qualification she sought to be a secondary school teacher, though, as one of the *professeurs agrégées*, a decidedly high rank of teacher.

Accordingly, Weil moved in August 1931 to Le Puy, south of Lyons, to take up a role as teacher of philosophy at the girls' *lycée*.

True to her political beliefs, Weil attempted to involve herself in the lives of ordinary workers. At Le Puy, while teaching, she threw herself into a period of political activism and in 1932 was the subject of a local Police Commissioner's report complaining about her propensity for fomenting revolt.

To some, Weil was an effective teacher. A letter survives from Anne Reynaud-Guerithault, one of her school students, in which she dismisses the notion that there were two Simone Weils, the premystical and the mystical. Reynaud-Guerithault argued that the careful attention to the logic of an argument, concern for the student, willingness to share what she had and capacity for witness were all qualities fully apparent in Weil's teaching days.[1] To others, however, she was careless with meeting school objectives or preparing students for examinations. Ultimately, Weil moved on from teaching.

The Great Depression in the 1930s affected France with the same severity with which it struck the rest of Europe. Although the more agile and responsive British economy had partially recovered from the Depression by 1936, the French economy had not and barely grew at all over the period 1929–39. The year 1934 was particularly difficult, with riots and mass unemployment in France's large manufacturing sector. Nor was France's tortured political system of much help, with different elements advocating either austerity to balance the budget or expenditure to raise purchasing power. Devaluation of the franc, in imitation of the actions of its trading partners, was resisted until 1937. The emergence of the Popular Front government in 1936, headed by Leon Blum, might have assisted in restoring growth and stability to the economy except that the amalgam of predominantly Leftist forces which comprised it could not agree on an economic strategy.

It was in 1934 that Weil took a year's leave of her teaching responsibilities then at the girls' lycée in Roanne (west of Lyons) to go and work as a factory hand. Her intellectual interest in testing experientially what factory work was like, rested on the notion of worker control. Worker control was one of the early slogans of the Bolsheviks and remained an issue of central importance to all parties of the Left outside the Soviet Union.

Weil was also moving towards the view that physical labor was authentic and spiritually ennobling. This engagement in labor was to be reprised later in her work with Gustav Thibon where she assisted in his vineyard before departing from France, but at this stage Weil was just experimenting. Her upbringing had been utterly bourgeois and her encounters with the lives of the ordinary working French had been minimal. Weil believed that trying to live the life of the working class was a necessary step if she was to write on working class issues with any sense of ownership.

Weil was, at that stage of her life, less a Communist than an anarcho-syndicalist. Anarcho-syndicalism was a movement among the Left, French in origin, which believed in worker control of the physical plant involved in production. It saw a minor role for the State, which it viewed as inextricably committed to the rights of property owners. Anarcho-syndicalism is distinguishable from Marxism (from which it split during the First International) in the matter of the leading role of the State. Anarcho-syndicalism's core commitment was to worker control and unions as an expression of such control. This set of political ideas explains much of Weil's political commitment at this stage of her life. To actualize this commitment required involvement in the lives of factory workers and in the work they undertook. Her physical frailty made this concrete involvement a difficult period for her but Weil persisted in her attempts to become one with the workers. Weil continued to contribute pieces of political ephemera to Left publications. This combination of Left political writing and identification with factory work was a common characteristic of political writers of the Left in the interwar years, not only in France. George Orwell, for example, took to the road and accepted bits of casual work as he travelled in order to understand the British unemployed. The result was *The Road to Wigan Pier*, his first successful piece of writing. Sinclair Lewis and John Steinbeck had a similar affection for the working poor. Like most intellectuals taking to factory work to identify with the workers, Weil was hopeless at the task, as her diaries note. She was, twenty-five years old.

As Weil had expected, factory work was repetitive, dehumanizing and boring.

> To speak frankly, for me this life is pretty hard, and the more so as my headaches have not been obliging enough to withdraw so as to make things easier. In a general way, the temptation to give up thinking altogether is the most difficult one to resist in a life like this: one feels so clearly that it is the only way to stop suffering. . . . One is left with no possible feeling about one's own fate except sadness.[2]

When laid off, Weil found other periods of work in factories, including ten weeks at the Renault factory, and continued to correspond with friends about factory work and its meaning for those forced to endure it.

Her concern for labor to have some dignity never left Weil and reentered her writings in her last work (*The Need for Roots*) in 1943. The experience of factory work changed her revolutionary views. Weil moved on from the Marxian notion of workers as the carriers of revolutionary consciousness to a view that factory work killed what was important in the person, leaving little consciousness for personal development or liberation.

Weil's factory experiences of humiliation, exhaustion and helplessness gave her a powerful metaphor—the slave. At the end of her experiment in factory work and prior to resuming her teaching responsibilities, Weil had a holiday with her parents in Portugal. Portugal at the time was an economically underdeveloped right-wing dictatorship and off the tourists' beaten track. It was a Europe with which she was totally unfamiliar. On her holiday in Portugal Weil came to the realization that Christianity was a religion of slaves, rather like the dispossessed proletariat with whom she had so recently worked. Perhaps Weil's sojourn among the worker "slaves" of industrial France actually did give her a profound insight into the nature of the person that she would not have acquired if she had remained a teacher: that Christ is there preeminently for wretched people. This image of the slave was, for her later thought, both potent and productive. Reflecting on the lessons derived from her factory stints, she wrote to her friend Albertine Thevenon linking factory work to slavery because of the need for the operator to work fast and to work in complete obedience, accepting the orders and abuse of the boss without demur.[3] She had found the work dehumanizing but this left open the question of what one could actually do about it.

After her Portuguese holiday, Weil left this question aside for the moment and returned to academic life, taking up a teaching appointment at the lycée of Bourges.

In May 1936 the Left in France formed a Popular Front Government comprising elements from among the Communists, Socialists and Social Democrats. It lasted until well into 1938, but was dissolved because of the insoluble differences of political opinion among elements of the Left with respect to the Spanish Civil War and the role to be played, if any, by France.

The Spanish Civil War had broken out in 1936 and it focused opinion in Europe on the choice in contemporary politics between Left and Right. The war was a *cause celebre* in Europe in the years leading up to to the Second World War because it was widely regarded as a proxy for the struggle between freedom, represented by the Republican side, and reaction, represented by the Nationalist or conservative side. It is generally the case that the winning side of a war gets to write the history. This has not been the case with the Spanish Civil War where the winning Nationalists tended to be branded with the reputation of being classic Right Wing thugs while the losing Republicans retained the aura of having lost the fight for democracy in Spain. This simplification has some merit. The Phalange, the Nationalist winners, were in fact a genuinely Right Wing movement—monarchist, anti-union, pro-property, anti-democratic and clerical. Once national elections had been narrowly won by the Left in 1936, the Right organized a military *coup* to topple the government and it was resistance to that coup which led to the three-year war. The Right saw itself as fighting against communism and atheism and in this they were largely correct. The Left, the Republican government of Spain, drew in a wide variety of fellow travelers to assist in its struggle, including socialists, anarchists, liberals and communist operatives from the Soviet Union who typically attempted to steer the course of the Civil War to their own ends. The widespread view among intellectuals at the time was that the Spanish Civil War was a kind of last chance to resist Fascism in the face of a looming European war. Despite the Leftist myth making, the Left, who actually got to write the history, proved merciless in their prosecution of the civil war, in their determination to root out any manifestation of religion and, eventually, any sign among their allies of deviation from the Communist Party line. The role of the Soviets in attempting to run the amalgam of Left forces, together with their particular brand of ruthlessness and brutality, were then as now routinely overlooked by academic historians, probably because these events were at the time poorly reported by a journalistic community fully embedded on the Republican side.

Following a stint of farm work, this time to learn the particular challenges of the agricultural workforce, Weil decided to go to Spain to join the struggle. Although still intellectually a pacifist, she went in 1936 as a volunteer helper with the Aragon anarcho-syndicalists in support of the Left or Republicans. Weil lasted only two months, the adventure ending in another embarrassing inability to carry out the mission she had set herself. Following a cooking accident Weil shipped back to France to recover and refocus. She returned to France disillusioned and looking for new intellectual frameworks in which to understand the powerful political forces abroad in Europe as it moved towards war.

It is difficult for us now to recapture the moral fervor and sense of outrage which was adrift in Europe in the days just before the beginning of the Second World War. The full force of the Nazi menace, about which the political class in Western Europe had been in denial, was at last manifest for all to see in 1938 and 1939, the years of the Munich Crisis and its aftermath, which culminated in the Nazi-Soviet Pact. The clash of Nazism and Communism, which had dominated the 1930s, had never been about the role of democracy, which had relatively few defenders in that period. Rather, it had been about the struggle for the soul of Socialism, widely seen as the political norm of the future. French politics had always been a struggle between a divided Left and a divided Right, but at this period the Left was attempting to form alliances with the Far Left, the Communists, in an attempt to meet the challenges of Nazism and Germany's attempt to overturn the Versailles settlement of 1919. Weil left behind her pacifism in this period as did many intellectuals in Europe, as the realization grew that France would once again be at war with Germany and that the country was militarily unprepared for the struggle.

Weil's views on the Left and its socialist path had already matured by the time she returned from Spain. Like many who had gone to Spain to fight for the Republic, she came to the realization that the achievement of the political program of the Left, as demonstrated in Spain, implied coercion, and coercion in turn was allied to slavery. For instance, an earlier essay of hers, *Towards the Proletarian Revolution* was an examination of Soviet Communism and its rule via a privileged *nomenklatura* where the worker, the ostensible subject of the revolution, had become instead the oppressed object.

The pattern of Weil's life in her midtwenties shows a search for meaning through identification with the poor and oppressed. The periods of low-paid factory and agricultural work, the flight to join the Republicans in Spain, the fact that she was not particularly good at any of these pursuits, all show a mind not remotely settled in her life's work. She published the occasional paper or article and remained close to her parents who seem to have accepted Weil's dilettantish approach to her career, probably because they shared the same liberal opinions. In retrospect, little of this was wasted. The lessons from these periods of Weil's life reentered her later writings time and again and although there appears little of system in her working life during these important years, she was absorbing insights, feelings and experiences which were to make for a high degree of wisdom in the truly remarkable period which lay before her.

Following her experience at Solesmes, the Benedictine monastery where she had gone to recover her health and where she had an experience of religious conversion, Weil entered a productive period of writing, producing through 1939 a number of essays on the nature of force with lessons from the world of the Greeks which she compared with the world of the Romans. She also wrote up her notebooks, a means by which she could put down her thoughts and play with ideas which had not yet reached maturity.

Much of Weil's thought during the crucial period, from just before the War broke out to her departure from France, is collected in a posthumously published volume, *Waiting for God*.[4] It is a collection of her writings executed prior to her departure and left with her friend and confidant Fr.J-M Perrin. These writings were a summation of her most important theological insights written after she had reached a sort of plateau of understanding and insight in her turbulent life. They are writings of one who wished to explain herself and to plead the reasonableness of her stance—a kind of *apologia* of her life. One reads them and recognizes their inherent integrity because Weil was not writing for any other person but to explain to herself what followed for her from her revelations.

WAR BREAKS OUT

The Second World War began on 3 September 1939 and France, together with Britain, was forced to honor its guarantee to Poland in the event of a German invasion. The French military forces were formidable on paper and highly focused on defensive operations. Essentially, they waited for a possible German attack until May 1940 when it eventually came. The costly and poorly conceived Maginot Line, designed to protect France's eastern border, was easily sidestepped by the Germans. The small British forces, together with significant French forces, were outmaneuvered in northern France and Belgium by a surprise incursion of German tank forces through the forested Ardennes region. Completely outflanked and poorly led, the British forces were out of the game and while most (329,000) were evacuated off the beaches of Dunkirk, the loss of equipment and their strategic failures meant that Britain would exercise no land role in the European War for years to come.

The French, meanwhile, also suffered from poor strategic preparedness. In the interwar years, they had focused their military resources on defense, in the belief that modern weaponry, tanks, aircraft and mechanized transport dictated the superiority of a defensive over an offensive stance. Notwithstanding the unfolding of the *blitzkrieg* in Poland, the French prepared themselves for a reprise of the previous war and by the time the Germans had rolled up the British Expeditionary Force on the beaches of Dunkirk, the French had lost any initiative. The French air force was poorly equipped. The French tank resources were large but widely dispersed and generally unavailable for massed attack as the Germans' were. Without coherent strategy, poor tactics and confused leadership at the top, the French too succumbed to the Germans in a matter of weeks.

The French Government evacuated Paris as the Germans approached. A horde of refugees took to the roads to evade the coming Germans and some six million French citizens uprooted themselves to attempt to find refuge elsewhere, fearful of a reprise of the 1914 situation. The rapid German defeat of France and the invasion of the country resulted in significant changes for France. With just under 100,000 soldiers killed and a further 1.8 million taken prisoner, Paris lost and confused refugees everywhere, the government, finally in Bordeaux, sought an armistice. Marshal Petain emerged as the new leader of the government and the French forces laid down their arms. France was divided into an occupied zone around the exposed sea borders and an unoccupied zone centered on Vichy where the new French government made its capital.

The French collapse was a moral failure as well as a military defeat. It became emblematic of the contradictions and moral vacuity of the Third Republic that it ended in a squalid flight from the capital. French resistance to the German advance through Belgium and thence through north eastern France was weak, even languid, with poorly trained troops and poorly conceived strategy. There was an absence of unity among the French political class which played into Hitler's hands as they argued not only the strategy but the purpose of the struggle. British attempts to shore up their ally's commitment produced no real results save for a lingering French shame which outlasted the War. The French kept their fleet at Toulon from which port it might have been used by either the French or the Germans to oppose France's former ally Britain. As a consequence of this evasion, the British sank it shortly after the armistice. French duplicity about the level of cooperation which the Petain regime was prepared to entertain, in the interests of liberating France, continued throughout the War. In the event, the Germans occupied the Atlantic and Channel coasts of France and key internal cities including Paris. The center of the continuing French government was to remain located in Vichy until the liberation of France in 1944.

SIMONE WEIL LEAVES FRANCE

On June 13, 1940, Weil accompanied her parents to Vichy and then to Marseilles *en route* to the USA where they expected to join her brother who had already left. While in Marseilles, she continued writing, this time for the opposition network now forming to counter the German occupation. Weil produced a work on the need for frontline nurses actually engaged in battle. The notion of women either fighting or supporting fighters on the frontline was new in Western Europe though it would become commonplace in the Soviet Union and, after the War, in Israel, thence universally. At the time of Weil's writing it seemed bizarre, especially in Vichy France which wanted nothing but peace, to keep its collective head down and to cooperate with the Germans until the War had passed.

A few months after arriving in Marseilles Weil wrote a famous, perhaps notorious, letter to the Vichy Ministry of Education, which had denied the rights of Jews to work. In this letter Weil denied that she was a Jew by race according to the law or by religion.[5] She concluded that if she had any religious tradition, it was Catholic. She clearly resented the denial by the regime of any capacity for her to work, especially as a professor, for which she was educated. She could not have been aware of the impending collaboration of the Vichy regime in the Final Solution, nor indeed of the fact of the Final Solution itself, then being hatched in Germany. The letter, brief and dashed off in a fit of pique as it was, remains incongruous in one so committed to the oppressed.

Before departing for the USA, Weil made the acquaintanceship of J-M Perrin, a Dominican priest with whom she entered into a dialogue about theology and the Church. Her correspondence with him was to become an important compendium of her thinking and a source for her biography. Through him she met Gustave Thibon, the farmer and pro-Petain writer for whom she went to work on land he owned (in a manner similar to her Renault experience) and with whom she was to lodge some of her most important writings prior to departing overseas. Later, reflecting on Weil's period with him, Thibon commented on her pervasive spirituality:

> in no other human being have I come across such familiarity with religious mysteries . . . she actually experienced in its heartbreaking reality the distance between knowing and knowing with all one's soul, and the one object of her life was to abolish that distance.[6]

The period following her sojourn with Thibon was highly productive, as far as Weil's writings were concerned. By this stage, her preoccupations were still theological although she continued to write on a variety of other subjects including the philosophy of science and Hellenistic culture. It is to this period in her life, just before she left for the USA, that Weil's conversion to the Church belongs, whether or not she actualized this commitment through baptism.

Together with her parents, Weil departed for the USA via Casablanca on May 14, 1942. She was reluctant to leave but felt unable to send her parents off unaccompanied. From her correspondence at this time, one gets the impression that Weil would have preferred to stay and die, possibly in the service of the frontline nursing unit of which she still wrote and which seems in retrospect to have been especially misconceived. But the course which the War later took was quite opaque at that period. The utter ghastliness of the War had not emerged in its full ferocity till 1941 growing worse as time progressed. Starting with the German invasion of Russia that year, the level of violence escalated to unprecedented levels. The Final Solution which was part of this escalating violence was not imagined in the middle of 1940 when the Germans invaded France, and the possible future complicity of the Vichy regime, ostensibly French and civilized, was inconceivable.

Weil reached New York on 8 July 1942 and set about journeying to Britain. Having obtained the permission of the provisional French government in London, she sailed for England and after a period of assessment by the authorities, settled in Notting Hill to work, via her writings, for the Free French authorities. Free to write without hindrance, alone in London where she could feel liberated to contribute to the war effort directly, and having some like-minded French around her, Weil proceeded to write an astonishing set of works including *The Need for Roots* on the future regeneration of France through a rediscovery of French cultural roots. She, along with others, had a vague desire to be parachuted back into France to work undercover. Given everything—her physical frailty, her lack of training for such an endeavor and her lack of any concrete reason for doing so—her request was turned down. Her unfocussed desires to be physically and immediately relevant to the war effort and the confused plans which arose from these, contrast sharply with the focus and intensity of her writings during this period. More than one commentator has concluded that she was simply courting death.

From January to August 1943 Weil remained in London working and writing. At this time she wrote *The Need for Roots*, her final work mentioned above, a treatise on the values which should inform a reemergent France following the War. She adopted the discipline of fasting, refusing to eat more than she imputed was available to the suffering French in order, vicariously, to share their travails. This period of Weil's life has been scrutinized in detail. Was she trying to die? Was she anorexic? What was the purpose of such extreme witness? Britain was under wartime rationing but there was no absolute shortage of food and many food items were available on an unrationed basis. In France, food was absolutely in short supply, given the obligation of the regime to supply Germany. But even in France the food shortages to which she pointed were uneven and mitigated by a vast black market. While France had food shortages, areas of the Soviet Union were literally starving. Like many who refused to be complicit, she saw the sufferings of France and experienced an existential inability to stand aside.

The last, productive year of her life ended in August 1943 in Kent, where Weil had been taken for rest and recuperation after a collapse. She died in a sanatorium in Kent of tuberculosis exacerbated by other conditions, including either malnutrition or diet.

Following her death, and once the War was finished, Weil's writings were gathered together and began to be published. These gathered writings included the manuscripts she left with Gustave Thibon in the south of France. He was an important part of her introduction to the world and, being one who knew her intimately, he was in a position to provide context to the published notebooks and essays.

AFTER THE WAR: HER WRITINGS

Weil had a publishing history prior to the discovery of her works after the War. Early works were published in Alain's *Libre Propos*. She was a regular contributor to *Les Cahiers du Sud* during her stay in the south of France following the occupation of Paris and prior to her departure to the USA. Weil's earlier writings (1931–36) cover a wide range of contemporary problems reflecting the particular political interests she had at the time. These included the plight of the poor, the unemployed and the factory worker. The writings that date from her inspired years (1938–43) focus overwhelmingly on religious faith, the nature of man, the encounter with God, the self-emptying of Christ and its consequences and the logic of the Cross. *Waiting for God* was a series of letters and essays put together after her death and contain her own explanation of her spiritual journey.

In *Gravity and Grace* (a representative sample of her theology first pulled together from writings and fragments and published in 1947 with an introduction by Gustave Thibon) Weil made a number of powerful and arresting assertions about God, man and their relationship—attachment creates illusion, reality depends on detachment, the creation of the universe involves a divine self-effacement. Grace, she said, is everywhere in the Void in which man dwells. It is contrasted with gravity, man's primitive moral underbelly. For Weil, gravity and grace were the two forces at work in the world and man must encounter God both within the Void and through a shroud of silence.

Weil's later *political* views were best expressed in the *The Need for Roots* (1949). This text, unlike her other works, was actually written as a book, or rather as a report, to the Free French authorities in London and as an aid in the political reconstruction of France. Her conclusion was that human communities faced the problem of uprootedness and a new humanism was needed to rectify that, a set of social relations, that is, based on the priority of obligation over rights and of work over all. Although Weil wrote the book in 1943 at the request of the London Free French and to make a practical contribution to the reconstruction of post-war France, it was sidelined largely because of the unevenness of the arguments and the highly original policy prescriptions. In *Oppression and Liberty* (1955) Weil had already covered the issues of individual and social freedom under different social arrangements reflecting largely the political thought forms of the late 1930s.

CONCLUSION

Since her death, Weil has never lost her power as observer and commentator on the human condition. She continues today to attract readers willing to wrestle with the very demanding categories with which she presented her insight (gravity, grace, Void, affliction, decreation, absence, attention). Both the starting point and the terminus of her argument was God in his relationship with man through the Cross and the self-emptying of Christ. Weil was certainly Catholic in sympathy as well as in practice but it is an open question whether she was ever baptized. That point is perhaps of no practical relevance (since one of the three categories of baptism in Catholic doctrine is baptism of desire) given that her total theological stance was Catholic. It is evident, however, that if she was Catholic, she was the black sheep of the Catholic family. Weil had a deep suspicion of the Church (and indeed of any collective); she regarded its level of religious practice and the depth of its real faith as largely illusory; she believed that the normal mode of intercessory prayer was contrary to the evidence of an absent God; she was distrustful of the Church's historic search of power and she especially criticized its incapacity to model itself after the self-emptying Christ.

Weil's later political thought (including her views on social policy) flowed entirely from her theology. Indeed, her signature work here, *The Need for Roots*, began with the needs of the soul and ended with the acceptance of work and death as true obedience to God. In this, Weil's overarching philosophy proved compelling but the practical implications she derived from it were less so. The Free French seem to have focused on the practical measures before rejecting the work in its entirety. Fortunately, the book survived and continues to draw in and beguile a wide range of social and political commentators intrigued by the far-seeing vision of one caught up in both the love of God and compassion for afflicted humanity, whose life Weil strove to share and to understand.

Weil's works still constitute a remarkable new way of speaking theology. There is a freshness and daring in her assertions and in the extreme individualism of her stance. This stance and its language quickly gained her a sympathetic audience within and outside the Christian community. In its focus and demands, this theology seems to speak more and more relevantly to our own century than to that in which it was written, a point we shall return to in chapter six. This is partly because we live in an age where God has been left to die. The silence of God, coupled with the consequences of the freedom of man to act in any way he wants, have proven too difficult for the current age to grapple with. Why not, therefore, a universe where all is accident and chance with nothing at all behind the veil of the silence of God, but silence? One of Weil's truly lasting contributions here has been a path through the default atheism of the age to a new set of assertions about the true nature of the divine *milieu* and to a more realistic interpretation of our own life in relation to the divine.

NOTES

1. Miles, Sian (ed). *Simone Weil an Anthology*. London: Penguin Classics, 2005 p12
2. Miles, S *Anthology* p20
3. Miles, S *Anthology* p27
4. Weil, Simone. *Waiting for God*. (Crawford E *trans*.) New York: Harper Perennial, 2009
5. Panichas *Reader* p79
6. Miles, S *Anthology* p40

Chapter Three

Encounter

THE HUMAN CONDITION

Weil's fame is in her writing and her life. In the last six years she wrote the works which form the permanent value of her writing corpus. Here, her life informed her writing and to a large extent her writing drove the vector of her life. Central to understanding Weil's significance to her own century and to ours, is our capacity to grasp the meaning of her encounter with the Other, that is her possession by the divine and to evaluate the manner in which it determined what she wrote and how she lived the rest of her life.

Much survives of Weil's writings prior to her experience of encounter and conversion, especially her extended analysis of oppression and liberty. These writings, largely gathered together from political ephemera which she published in the 1930s were first published in English in book form in 1955.[1] Reading them, the extent of her subsequent intellectual journey becomes clear. Generally speaking, her early writings formed an extended analysis of liberty, social oppression, freedom, revolution and progress from a Marxian perspective. Her insight into revolution was sharp but much of the rest is now of limited use in evaluating her final views on force, power, freedom and the individual. Her early writing set the point from which her definitive intellectual journey really began.

Of more interest is her work on the meaning of the Iliad, published in *Cahiers du Sud* in 1940–41, where she dwelt on the Greek genius for defining and lamenting the human condition, a flowering of literature carried over, centuries later, into the gospels. Contemplating the epic of the Iliad and later Attic tragedy, Weil concluded that Greek tragedy was pervaded by the overarching theme of justice. The countervailing theme of might appeared time and again as a cold and unflinching intrusion. Might produced fatal outcomes and nobody could escape them. It was to Greek tragedy that her discovery of *affliction* could be traced. Affliction was the humiliation of the soul that intensified and heightened the sufferings of the body and Greek tragedy did not seek to veil or disguise such abject abandonment. It even included the capacity to admire the hero who is disdained. So it is, in Weil, with the four gospels that tell the story of Christ as the suffering and abandoned one. They were, in her rendition, the last expression of the Greek genius for exposing the extent and reality of human suffering as captured in the life of the hero who is the victim of might.

> The accounts of the passion show that a divine spirit united to the flesh is altered by affliction, trembles before suffering and death, feels himself at the moment of deepest agony separated from men and from God.[2]

This segue from Greek literature to the Christian gospels was of a piece with Weil's spirituality. In the Iliad, so she argued, the dominant theme was the operation of force in the world. By the workings of balance or equilibrium in the world, Achilles failed to appreciate the operation of nemesis or retribution: both triumph and failure came to every hero and only nemesis ultimately won. Although the gods of the Iliad were beyond human control, humans were tempted to believe that they could control the gods whereas, in fact, there was no real security in the hero's strength.

Heroes strove for prestige, which presumed force. As in the Iliad, the gods being in control meant that prestige was illusory; control was only an appearance. The loss of prestige, the realization of a total lack of control over the circumstances of one's life, Weil defined as *affliction*. She dealt with this in detail in a further essay on *The Human Personality*. Here, she pointed out that in normal modes of thought, the person was unable to acknowledge the reality of affliction, a rending of the body and an abandonment of the soul. Affliction was terrible because it threatened the random loss of everything the person held dear in life, including the things which the person considered as constituting his or her being: "There is nothing that I might not lose. . . .To be aware of this in the depth of one's soul is to experience non-being."[3]

This was part of Weil's understanding of the human condition. It was also part of her understanding of the passion of Christ who, in affliction, lost all prestige and died as an abandoned criminal. Christ's death was not that of a hero nor a martyr: it was that of an object of disgust, which was why the resurrection was the signature of God. Just as the hero's prestige rested on the recognition of others, so the vindication of Christ the anti-hero rested on public disdain. Weil's understanding of the nature of the person developed after her religious conversion.

PERSONAL CONVERSION

Weil's personal conversion opened to her a number of insights which were centered on love and based on the excising of the personal from the personality. By her own account, this conversion to Christianity involved a number of steps. In 1937 Weil had long and repeated periods of absence from teaching in an attempt to regain the health which was in a constant state of deterioration. The year also saw her continue to write on the question of work and labor relations as well as the increasingly important subject of war. Weil began work in Picardy teaching Philosophy and Greek at the lycée Saint Quentin, using this position as a base to extend and deepen her political writings. She took a further holiday to Switzerland and then to Assisi in Italy. She spent two days in Assisi and took the opportunity to visit the famous chapel (Santa Maria deli Angeli) where St. Francis used to pray. It was during this stay that, as she said, that "something stronger than I was compelled me for the first time in my life to go down on my knees."[4]

The following year Weil took sick leave from January to June (her headaches again) and went to the town of Solesmes, northeast of Paris, to the Benedictine monastery to rest. During this period she made the acquaintanceship of a young English man who introduced her to the poetry of George Herbert, one of the English metaphysical poets. She was particularly struck by his poem, Love:

> Love bade me welcome; yet my soul drew back
> Guilty of dust and sin.
> But quick-eyed Love, observing me grow slack
> From my first entrance in
> Drew nearer to me, sweetly questioning
> If I lack'd anything.
>
> "A guest" I answer'd "worthy to be here."
> Love said, "You shall be he."
> "I, the unkind, the ungrateful? Ah my dear,
> I cannot look on Thee."
> Love took my hand and smiling did reply,
> "Who made the eyes but I?"
>
> "Truth, Lord: but I have marred them: let my shame
> Go where it doth deserve."
> "And know you not," says Love, "Who bore the blame?"
> "My dear then I will serve."
> "You must sit down," says Love, "and taste my meat,"
> So I did sit and eat.

It was at Solesmes, during the recitation of the poem as prayer that, Weil reported, Christ "took possession" of her. She said that she learned the poem by heart and that it became a kind of prayer for her. It was during the recitation of this prayer that her "possession" occurred. She described it as a real contact between God and herself: in the midst of suffering there was the presence of Love and neither her senses nor imagination had any part in it. Her intellectual problems about the existence and action of God in the world were subsumed in an experience of encounter, unsought and inexplicable. She had not come across this phenomenon before: "God in his mercy had prevented me from reading the mystics, so that it should be evident to me that I had not invented this absolutely unexpected contact."[5] It is this sudden, unexpected and unsought "possession" that characterizes the phenomenon of spiritual consolation, an emotion or experience Weil shared with the mystics whom she reported she had not read. St. Ignatius of Loyola, one of these mystics, provided a parallel report:

> Consolation (is) an interior movement in the soul by which it is inflamed with love of its . . . Lord . . . when one sheds tears which move to the love of God . . . (or) every increase in faith, hope or love and all interior joy that invites and attracts . . . to the salvation of one's soul by filling it with peace and quiet in its Lord.
>
> God alone can give consolation to the soul without any previous cause. It belongs solely to the Creator to come into a soul to draw it wholly to the love of (himself).[6]

At this point in her life Weil began to pray, finding ways to ensure that her attention was fixed on the one being encountered. Her eventual conclusion was that prayer, properly understood, was attendance, or attention, or waiting—complete focus on the one being communicated with. Silence was the essence, but in that silence was the experience of positive relationship. If noises intruded, they were perceived as coming across a void of silence. Silence and infinity were the realm of prayer. She reported,

> sometimes, during this recitation or at other moments, Christ is present with me in person, but his presence is infinitely more real, more moving, more clear than on that first occasion when he took possession of me.[7]

These experiences seem to have formed Weil's view of both the human condition and the spiritual reality of the human personality. The language with which she emerged—decreation, the impersonal, withdrawal and so on—implies a different sort of active involvement with the world, commitment without the imposition of force and an accentuation of the impersonal aspect of the soul over the personal, the "I."

Simultaneously with her conversion, Weil became a theological writer with a startling capacity to surprise and shock without losing her commitment to social and political writing. By the time she left France in May 1942, Weil had formed and developed a deeply grounded theology of the Cross, fully reflective of the theology of St Paul but written and explicated in her own unique style. Like Kierkegaard, whom we know she had read, she saw Christianity not as an institution where faith was a possibility depending on conformity of one sort or another, but rather as a way of seeing reality. That reality was a Void where the encounter in faith had to be managed in silence and by the individual. Weil's model of the encounter of faith was one where the soul was touched by God, even if briefly, who then deserted it and let it struggle over the remainder of its life searching for him through this Void. As the soul struggled to retain the sense of encounter, God, from the other side struggled to find and retain the soul. This double search constitutes a type of reenactment of the meaning of the Cross. It is a complex model but it reflects the type of life which Weil was to live out as a Christian. The soul needs only that one moment of illumination—and hers was at Solesmes—and it has the basis of communion with a God who is otherwise silent. Meaning, for her, is in the search which is ongoing, struggling to recapture and intensify the initial encounter. The intense effort that has to be put into recapturing the initial revelation over the rest of one's life demands attention to God and this attention constitutes prayer.

PERSONAL AND IMPERSONAL

What of the person? Weil started with the idea that when we look at the person, it is not the personal which is sacred but the impersonal. Just as the social prestige of the hero turned out to be illusory in the Greek epic, given that the gods were in charge and they were prone to act in a manner which was random, so for Weil the admired achievements of science, literature and human endeavor were mere manifestations of personality, which gifts in turn were bestowed randomly. The highest things in humanity were achieved far from this petty realm. They were achieved by people anonymously, their names probably lost forever and with no lasting personality, because they had no fame. Truth and beauty belonged in this upper realm of the impersonal. The example she proposed was the child completing a sum. If the sum is completed incorrectly, it is a mark of the personality; if correctly, the personality has no relevance. The *im*personal was the mark of perfection. "Perfection," as she put it "is impersonal. . . . The whole effort of the mystic has always been to become such that there is no part left in his soul to say 'I.'"[8]

For Weil, this "impersonal" was reached by attention which came with solitude. It could be done by the individual, but not by the collective, which was the enemy of the impersonal. The impersonal and the attendant individuality had to be fought for. It followed that, in order to seek perfection, the individual had to escape from the collective and the personal into the realm of the impersonal. When that happened, there was a part of the soul which the collective could not touch. If the person's soul was rooted in the impersonal then that person could draw energy from that fact. The act of clinging to the impersonal generated real force which would enable the individual to challenge the collective should the moral need arise. Moreover, the collective needed such connections to the impersonal.

> There are occasions when an almost infinitesimal force can be decisive . . . every collectivity depends for its existence on operations which can only be performed by a mind in a state of solitude.[9]

In later works, her hostility to the collective would surface in Weil's views on one particular collective—the political party. In the background, as well, were both her ambiguous attitude to the church and her reluctance to become one of its members. This individualism also helps to explain Weil's view of prayer as total attention, a relationship of complete focus on the Other.

Greek philosophy, from which Weil drew her inspiration, had a strong commitment to individual self-realization, expressed by the notion in modern personalist psychology of the uniqueness of the individual person, or consciousness or soul. Weil's contribution at this point was to extend the analysis of the individual by extreme contrast to the collective. This was not entirely an original argument: many others in nineteenth century European philosophy, including Kierkegaard, had emphasized the centrality of the individual against the crowd. But her reemphasis of this point opened up Weil's analysis of spirituality to the one-to-one relationship of the individual to God without reference to the church as well as the observation in passing that atheism could well be a stage of faith for those who might instinctively be worshipping God (via their actions) in his impersonal aspect.

For Weil, generalizing from her own experience, the encounter with God was individual and unmediated. It began as a relationship of mutual forgiveness, somewhat in the way of human relationships. The creation within which the human person lived represented something of a surrender by God, a partial retreat where God remained waiting for the free person to approach and love.

GRAVITY AND GRACE

The first and unpolished outline of Weil's unique experience was crystallized in *Gravity and Grace*, first published in 1947.[10] This was a text put out before scholarly work had begun on the scope and meaning of Weil's theology taken as a whole, so it strikes the reader as somewhat raw. It comprised a series of startling assertions formed as elaborate and provocative metaphors which captured Weil's personal experience of encounter with the Other and made it comprehensible to the implied reader. At the center of this theological construction was the individual who confronted death within a world in which a silent and hidden God revealed himself to anyone who sought, even if the person was unconscious of the search save for occasional brief flashes of insight. The world, in her theology, contained a Void, a primal emptiness which evidenced its need for God. This emptiness of God pointed to evil in the world because where God was not, evil could exist. God had not so much left the world, as it were, as withdrawn to allow man to exist and seek. What he must seek was Truth, which involved enduring the Void of life and facing death. Every soul was challenged to endure the Void and find that which lies beyond—the other life of God. Life was essentially a risk.

> Truth is on the side of death. Man only escapes from the laws of this world in lightning flashes. Instants when everything stands still, instants of contemplation, of pure intuition, of mental void, of acceptance of the moral void. It is through such instants that he is capable of the supernatural.[11]

DETACHMENT AND SUFFERING

In Weil's spirituality, detachment was necessary. This meant ceasing to try to control or escape the universe whether through force or through the consolations of religion. Detaching oneself from everything and waiting was the way of faith and the way that led to encounter. One had to learn to love God across and through the ghastliness of the world and the violence of its history, to be attached to nothing and to recognize one's own affliction in one's attachment to things. God would find the one who was detached and open to him, whether that soul believed in him or not. As she succinctly put it, "If we love God while thinking that he does not exist, he will manifest his existence."[12]

For Weil, suffering was inevitable and affliction had degrees. God was present in affliction and especially where the ego had been deliberately shrunk. Suffering may even have been redemptive where allied to evil.

The center and model of Weil's notion of the self in the world was that of Christ who emptied himself of his divinity and again, in the cross, of his humanity. The self emptying of Christ she saw as an unavoidable invitation to every soul, part of the logic of facing the Void. We were all born, she said, with a kind of false divinity (the personal) which we needed to shed by acknowledging that ultimately we were nothing. Once we reached this level of self understanding it should actually have become our object in life, to become that which we were: nothing.

> It is for this that we suffer with resignation, it is for this that we act, it is for this that we pray.
> "Except the seed die." It has to die in order to liberate the energy it bears within it.[13]

A further argument of Weil was that if evil was a natural accompaniment to creation, so suffering was an inescapable characteristic of the created world. As such, she concluded that suffering should be embraced as should other natural characteristics of the world we live in. Affliction, which Weil characterized as the end point of suffering, was made real and intensified by time and its passage.

> Time bears the thinking being in spite of himself towards that which he cannot bear and which will come all the same. "Let this cup pass from me." Each second which passes brings some being in the world nearer to something he cannot bear.[14]

But affliction opened us to knowledge and knowledge could be obtained only in suffering. The end point of suffering, as in Greek drama, was affliction, the point of suffering where the humiliation of the body was accompanied by the dereliction of the soul, a dereliction which drove out all that constituted the person's link with the divine. The mystery of Christ incorporated the fact that he too, in affliction, experienced God only as total abandonment. This stage of privation in affliction was where God was most present.

> This stage has to be reached if there is to be incarnation. The whole being becomes privation of God: how can we go beyond? After that there is only the resurrection. To reach this stage the cold touch of naked iron is necessary.[15]

Suffering and joy were, in Weil, complementary. One enhanced the other and the one who knew joy suffered all the more in affliction. Without joy, she said, life was just a bad dream. The ability to experience joy opened the person to the deep experience of suffering. By analogy, experiencing life and loving it, opened the person to the love of death.

> We must attain the knowledge of a still further reality in suffering, which is a nothingness and a void. In the same way we have greatly to love life in order to love death still more.[16]

SUFFERING, DEATH, AND EVIL

What should we make of the confronting possibilities which Weil opened up here in her analysis of the context within in which we live our lives and the meaning of the great negators—suffering and death—which deface our lives? In the rich and developed world, we live in an era where God is a redundant thesis and questions about the *meaning* of suffering and death are themselves regarded as meaningless. The entirely accidental universe within which we grasp at a totally contingent life, needs no further explanation than the laws of physics operating in a cosmos where there is no such thing as nothing. This was Weil's view in her materialist phase, which made all the more remarkable her transition to belief and her attempt to reconcile what was known about the chance creation of the universe with the reality of the God who lay beyond it. Weil's views and inferences seem to align well with a rational understanding of the world with no attempt to undermine science and acknowledging that God's life, as it were, was quite separate from ours and, though we had a material origin, God did not.

Weil's metaphor of the Void and the place of suffering lead us to a view of the radical elevation of the individual over the collective both in discerning meaning and discovering the divine. Where she examined suffering and death, she was entering the territory of the most profound importance. Weil's approach to the problem of evil—how an omnipotent God could allow human suffering—was to lay out for us the interaction of God and man in order to see the place of both suffering and death. God's creation, she said, involved a retreat of which the Incarnation was an extension. The Void of God's retreat created the space within which we had the capacity to approach God. Evil occupied the space as it must, the Void being that which was not God. But the Void was the locus for our encounter with God and our reaching for him was counterbalanced by his reaching for us. We may not even have realized we were reaching for God but our actions may have signified that we knew him in his non-personal aspect. The capacity for the individual to venture into the Void, to seek and be found by God was a form of grace. For Weil, the relationship between creature and creator across a Void of evil and death was exemplified in the life of Christ, who carried through to the end the logic of his relationship to the Father in the midst of affliction where the soul believed itself to be abandoned. This self-emptying was central to the importance of sufferings: they were for the purpose of fully realizing our life.

In some ways, Weil's approach was a radical simplification of the problem of evil. There was much that she omitted while failing to solve many of the problems inherent in it. That is largely because she was speaking from her apprehension of her own experience. Nor does Weil say that she was discussing the problem of evil. But in reflecting on her own conversion, this set of explanations—suffering, affliction, Void, encounter, grace, death—unpacked, for her at least, the enigma of the silence of an absent God in a universe pervaded by grace, but evil as well.

The universe in which we found ourselves, Weil said, was devoid of mercy and to suppose a beneficent universe was an illusion. The mystics, she noted, believed that, notwithstanding the pervasiveness of suffering in the world, the world itself was benign, a work of the mercy of God. They mistook God's mercy for them individually as pointing to creation itself as a realm of providential mercy. The reality of the world, however, should not be clouded over by illusion. The nature of the world was harsh.

> But as for obtaining evidence for this mercy directly from nature, it would be necessary to become blind, deaf and without pity in order to believe such a thing possible.[17]

The infinite mercy of God, God's providence properly understood, was actually behind the curtain of his profound silence. To imagine that there was no ultimate mercy, or that there was no curtain of silence separating us from that could only lead to the morally reckless intrusion of force. For Weil, the suffering of this world, apart from being inevitable, relentless and universal, served a function in forcing us to the view that we are nothing. If we labored under the illusion that somehow suffering was a trial sent to test us, we should fall under the parallel illusion that we amounted to something in the universe. Suffering, by contrast, demonstrated that we were nothing and it was only through suffering that we could come to see Truth and love God. Suffering was ultimately redemptive because it had the potential to open us up to the grace of God. In suffering, the person turned his gaze to the Other and meets the already turned gaze from the other side. This response, which is grace, is the singular and only favor of God.[18]

Weil's views on suffering have been labeled self-lacerating and masochistic but a careful reading of her work shows that she did not seek suffering nor did she wallow. Rather, the existence of suffering was one of the basic facts of the world she lived in and she knew this partly from her own illnesses, partly from her factory work and partly through the observation, without illusion, of the world's reality. Weil wrote always with people at the margins in mind, the laboring, struggling majority whom the political parties purported to represent but whom they never encountered. In evaluating Weil's views on suffering and affliction, and abstracting them from their historical context, one has to accept that she invoked a state of suffering that she believed people experienced as part of a general alienation in the world. This alienation pointed to the non-inclusion she inferred that everyone felt as a result of their need for human contact and their inability to achieve it. Affliction, for Weil, was beyond suffering. Affliction characterized the experience of Christ. Christ's death involved a complete self-emptying, that is, rejection and ridicule to the point of abandonment by God. The abandoned utterance of the soul at the end point of affliction encountered the silence of God: such was the path of affliction. It was to this end, rather than the resurrection that the christology of Weil pointed.

THE PERSON AND GOD IN ENCOUNTER

Weil's *Gravity and Grace* was collected and published from the fragments she left behind in France. Like all her works, it is unfinished, but it gives us an insight into her mind as it produced assertion after assertion each trying to grasp with greater precision her vision of the drama of the encounter between man and the divine. In *Gravity and Grace*, Weil used a language partly new and partly old. Among these were two basic concepts, gravity, which was unique to her and grace, which has always been a standard biblical category. In Weil's treatment, gravity was the tendency of human beings to sink beneath the level of the morally possible in themselves. It was the quality which led the person away from living an authentic life. Gravity was baseness; gravity was causing pain to others. The force opposing this was grace and that came from outside man, from another realm, as it were. The definition of grace has a long history, but it can be characterized traditionally as the immanence of God, the fact of the presence of God and the degree to which this is effective in our lives. In Weil, grace, this moral energy, was found outside ourselves, but mistakenly believed to have been found within ourselves because it had happened so easily. Although the universe was characterized by grace, the world had moved beyond realizing this, had outgrown any reliance on its pervasiveness and opted instead for what was superficial. In Weil's view, God's action in the world was constituted by grace alone, not, as was commonly understood, his physical intrusion into the lives of individuals. The capacity of the person to be moral and to rise to the call of grace was an optimistic aspect of her view of the human condition. This interplay of gravity and grace in both the unfolding of human history and grace's contradictory movements within the human soul are essentially the framework by which Weil's work can be understood.

THE INDIVIDUAL

In Weil's view, religious faith assisted in explaining the world and its history. For her, it especially assisted in explaining suffering and affliction by casting them as a necessary quality of the relationship between God and man. Faith followed from encounter which in turn only required search. The search was a task for the individual soul.

At the heart of this framework of gravity and grace was the human soul, the radically self-conscious individual who was the point of human history. One of the glories of Western philosophy was the conceptualization of the individual, differentiated from the collective and building social structures to protect and foster individuality. The notion of the individual arose from the observation that every person had the capacity to reason and hence to exercise free will. Free will gave the person the capacity to be ethically self-responsible. Weil affirmed this supremacy of the individual over the collective. It was the individual, the "I" who could undertake the call to self-emptying which for her was the basis of the relationship with the Other. This personality, to the extent that he or she could empty self, could be open to the ingress of grace which came to the person from outside: "Everything without exception which is of value in me comes from somewhere other than myself, as a loan which must be ceaselessly renewed."[19]

Weil's views on the centrality of the individual in her spirituality have several important antecedents, especially the radical individuality of Kierkegaard. We know that Weil was familiar with the Danish theologian: his influence can be discerned in much of her basic approach. Even though she used a different language, there is considerable overlap between Weil's views and Kierkegaard's. They include the primacy of the individual over the crowd, the centrality of faith, (the idea that God is known subjectively and on the basis of no evidence other than the subjective), the nature of commitment as a form of passion (of which enduring suffering and affliction were, for her, two negative forms), the pervasiveness of grace and the limited role of dogma in Christian faith.

Additionally, Weil's spirituality was absolutely centered on the self-emptying into powerlessness of God (in the Incarnation). For her, this self-emptying led to powerlessness and explained her view that Christianity, therefore, stood in opposition to religions of power.

Self-emptying has its origin in the theology of St. Paul. In Greek, the word is *kenosis* and he introduced the idea in his letter to the Philippians.

> Hold to this consciousness, the same as you have in Christ Jesus, who, though he was in the form of God, did not count his equality with God as something to cling to, but emptied himself by taking the form of a slave and being born in human form. And being born in human form he lowered himself further and became obedient to the point of death, actually death on a cross.[20]

This *kenosis* of God took place in the Incarnation and in the crucifixion as well, this being the end point of affliction. Weil's spirituality really started with the *kenosis* of the cross, an act akin to God's own partial self-renunciation or decreation. In imitation, one was called to de-create or renounce or empty oneself of the false divinity with which people regarded themselves. Furthermore, *kenosis* was the absolutely authentic response to the universal rule of force. She looked to the image of the grain of wheat which, in the gospel of John fell to the ground and died in order to yield a harvest. It was God's withdrawal that interested Weil, the capacity of God to make room, as it were, for the human being to encounter him. This retreat she captured in the idea of decreation, an insight which opened the way for people to share in the act of the cross, by becoming nothing, by renouncing everything.

PRIVATION

Weil argued that privation may be part of decreation but even this could contribute to the *re*-creation of the world. Privations were a test of endurance and pointed to the resilience of the soul. They had a more important use as well. For the individual, they pointed towards the testimony of human misery, the knowledge of which liberated from the carapace of illusion. Affliction could never be too extreme nor the abasement to which it lowered those who endured it because it opened the person to the knowledge of human misery, "knowledge which is at the door of all wisdom."[21]

If the knowledge of misery was at the heart of human wisdom, the way to it was through *kenosis*. To come to a true divinity we needed to shake off the false divinity which, in Weil's spirituality, was the thing of which we needed to empty ourselves. For her, false divinity was the self-regard, which put each of us in the center of a tiny universe of our own. But the real center of the world—everyone's world—was outside the world, behind the curtain and wrapped in the silence of God. Acknowledging that the real center of the world was outside the scope of our wisdom and actions meant accepting this world as it was because we could not change the laws of the universe but only exercise free choice in that single area which we controlled, within our own souls.

For Weil, the false divinity of our ego, as long as we maintained it, was a denial of the real nature of the relationship between God and the person. Humanity, in Weil's construction, was what was furthest from God, utterly other than God, the extreme limit of distance from God, from which it was just possible to come back. Metaphorically, the human soul was the crucifixion of God whose love for humanity was a passion. Such love meant that God was, in a sense, torn, loving that which was adrift in evil.

> How could that which is good love that which is evil without suffering? And that which is evil suffers too in loving that which is good. The mutual love of God and man is suffering.[22]

For Weil, the relationship between God and Man, the distance separating them was vast but such relationship was made possible by the act of God's *kenosis*. God as a crucified slave (St. Paul's image), someone looked down upon, demonstrated for us the vast distance between ourselves and God, our apprehension of distance, that is, being better imagined in a downward direction. The *kenosis* gave us an image by which we could capture the extent and nature of the love of God. "It is much easier for us to imagine ourselves in the place of God," as she put it, "than in the place of Christ crucified."[23]

This "infinite thickness" as Weil called it, which separated the person from God was also the distance to which both evil and love could extend. Through this "thickness" God comes—and waits. He came through the Incarnation and again through the cross, through self-abnegation and through affliction. The innocence of God wrestled with the reality of human evil and in this human universe, God made himself powerless because he was perfect. This drama of divine encounter exposed us to the actual reality of God. The innocent person who suffered served to bring salvation to evil. Such was the meaning of the image of the innocent God who encountered man and suffered. We could imagine God as powerful or as perfect, but not both. The logic of innocent suffering because of love connected God to man and *vice versa* with the way of perfection being the way of innocence.

> To be innocent is to bear the weight of the entire universe. It is to throw away the counterweight. In emptying ourselves we expose ourselves to all the pressure of the surrounding universe.[24]

The reality of God as self-emptying searcher, the reality of the world as suffering, the reality of evil and the silence of God: such were the building blocks of Weil's spirituality. Of the different stages of the development of Christian spirituality, her development was a demanding one but it derived from a realistic appraisal of human suffering. It is difficult, for example, to find continuity between Weil's writing and the optimistic spiritualities of both St John of the Cross or St Theresa or even the muscular and no-nonsense approach of Ignatius of Loyola: that is, until a consideration of two things. First, unlike the others, Weil began with an extensive description of the reality of the world and its suffering-to-the-point-of-affliction before venturing to describe what might follow from that in terms of encounter within this world.

In her view, suffering and evil had to be faced and defined before we could consider how to approach a God who had subjected himself to these. Secondly, people in our times understand the world in a way vastly different from the perspective of the Renaissance or the Middle Ages. Far from being controlled by an omniprovident God, as was universally held in the middle ages and through the Renaissance, in Weil, the nature of the world was that God had retreated to allow man to be man. God's silence was a necessary fact and man had to allow himself to be found through silence and listening, through suffering and, in the first place at least, alone.

NO ILLUSIONS

Clearly, Weil's view of human existence was profoundly pessimistic. Having lived through the war of 1914–18 and through some of the war of 1939–45, she was fully aware of the action of unleashed evil, or force, in the world. She was also aware of the lesser evils that beset ordinary people, especially the manipulation of the ignorant by the political class, the ruination of culture, the deracination of communities and the oppression of colonies and their Asian or African inhabitants in the pursuit of national glory. Weil knew patriotism and its folly, the undermining of education, the propensity of politics to resort to force and the corruption of the judicial system. She covered these and more in passing in her writings. Indeed it was from contemplating the sorrowful state of the world that Weil began her analysis in *The Need for Roots* with an exploration on the basic needs of the soul as a kind of preliminary to discussing social order and whether the social order should address people's spiritual needs.

The world Weil saw was a wasteland pervaded by both evil and grace, the first perfectly obvious, the second to be discerned. Weil believed that the political and social abandonment of the world could be redeemed by the capacity of the person to turn his or her gaze to God, whether consciously or unconsciously, and meet the already-turned gaze of God. Such is the manner, Weil believed, in which the searching person began to find God across the complexities of the times they lived in and the space they occupied. If we lived in a perfect world where there was no suffering, no hatred and no violence, we would be living in a world where the encounter with God would be unnecessary. But the real world was pervaded by an evil which was the derivative of God's necessary withdrawal from it in order to create the space for us to be.

Weil's extensive analysis of politics and the social order, much of which was undertaken prior to her conversion experience, eventually came together in her writings when she fused her concern for the deep sacredness of the human individual with the mysticism of her final days. The origins of evil were many, but the seeming inevitability of force in human affairs was, in her view, primary. This tendency for the world to be dominated by the preponderance of force was obvious to her in contemporary history, most immediately in Nazi aggression. It was also apparent in past history and its epic literature and in the differing cultures, both ancient and modern, which gave testimony to that. Weil's mysticism gained from her complete lack of illusion about the real state of force in the world and among humanity. What she discerned, despite the violent outcome for brute force in the world, was the impersonal sacredness of the individual. This sacredness within the individual was what allowed consent to the love of God, initiated, as it were, from the other side of the curtain.

In Weil's understanding of the human condition, the lessons from epic literature, the long standing traditions of human institutions and the beneficent products of civilizations all assisted in mediating the supernatural, since people were not just souls, but embodied entities who acted within known and understood frameworks. Because these traditions and products of the past, these artifacts of human culture, were so valuable they had to be protected from humans' propensity for escalating violence. They needed to be preserved because they formed a connection with the supernatural. Human violence, that is, would ultimately destroy the capacity of the person to be in any sense spiritual and to discover the pervasiveness of grace.

PRAYER

For Weil, prayer was an act of waiting while being as empty of self as possible even when the person's longing was inchoate, undefinable. Prayer was encounter: prayer was relationship: prayer was response to a movement initiated beyond the person.

Repeatedly Weil insisted that the action involved in prayer was attention and attention was waiting. At the heart of the love of God was this attention and waiting and it was the quality which was also at the heart of the love of neighbor. Attention was beyond warmth and pity: it was withdrawal to allow the other to enter. This attention involved desire and consent.

The soul hungered for knowledge of God because the limitations of the world were too apparent. Knowledge could only come with attention to what is real. Shorn of illusions, for Weil, every person was really aware that, for all the joy that one might encounter in the world, there was something vital missing. There was no good in the world that one could describe as absolute or final. People had the capacity of realizing this from time to time but they reverted to form and fell back to comfortable self deceptions. But to grapple with the existential randomness and sadness of existence and to use this struggle for good, we had to commit ourselves to the love of truth. We had to learn to love truth more than life itself. People failed to turn to God in the darkness generated by the unbearable suffering of life because they did not imagine that there could be anything but darkness. But God had already set their face in the right direction and if they remained motionless and listened intently and waited, the beginnings of a new intuition would emerge.

> If after a long period of waiting God allows them to have an indistinct intuition of his light or even reveals himself . . . it is only for an instant. Once more they have to remain still, attentive, inactive, calling out only when their desire cannot be contained. . . . It does not rest with the soul to believe in the reality of God if God does not reveal this reality.[25]

Encounter, in Simone Weil, occurred when the soul waited and listened. Prayer as attendance or attention occurred whether the other was human or divine. Attending to God was done in silence, in humility and with the consciousness of the infinity which separated: "We can only know one thing about God: that he is what we are not."[26]

Prayer as relationship in encounter did not need dogma nor church. It was what it purported to be—relationship—that is, connection first and foremost with one who was absent. This impelled towards good and may have led the individual anywhere, even to the Cross.

FAITH AS DECREATION AND ACCESS TO THE DIVINE SIDE OF THE CURTAIN

The person purified self through an act of what Weil called, as we have seen, decreation. The ego had to be stripped, reduced to allow the person to be conscious of the pervasiveness of something else in the universe that it was not—grace. Every person was burdened with a kind of protective layer, an imaginary divinity which put the self at the center of consciousness. Peeling away that ego opened the self up to the reality that at the time lay hidden because of the human ego: "An imaginary divinity has been given to man so that he may strip himself of it as Christ did of his real divinity."[27]

For Weil, decreation of the self helped us to establish our real self in a supernatural universe which the ego would normally obscure. Thus decreation was also an act of real creation because it led us to possess that which was the only thing, ultimately, that counted, God. We were nothing and should have striven for the realization that we were nothing. Prayer needed therefore to be directed at attempting to reduce and annihilate the ego, that is, decreation of the self.

COMPREHENDING OUR OWN REALITY

Decreation, *kenosis* and withdrawal were all at the heart of Weil's spirituality and it is worth asking how useful they are in comprehending our own existential reality. Her approach of argument-to-the-extreme was confronting and in some respects bewildering. If the first derivative of Christian faith was, as she held, eliminating the centrality of self, (the self, incidentally, that formed the relationship with the divine that *was* faith), what would be the point of so one-sided a relationship? To appreciate Weil's stance here, we need to understand that for her God's reality was greater than and preceded our own. The divine relationship was love and the first form of love was that of God for himself. Ultimately, it neither added to nor subtracted from God whether one had faith or not. What counted was that one came to the realization of the complete self-sufficiency of God for whom the creation was an act of self-surrender. To do that, one had to strive for decreation because the consciousness of self just got in the way.

For Weil, decreation was what could lead to occupying the same world as God. This reasoning led her to discount the notion of the immortality of the soul, or at least our conception of it, notwithstanding its being an article of faith in the Church and indeed part of the basis of Christianity's historical attractiveness. Weil said that we were not able to conceive of the soul in anything but bodily manner, which reduced the notion of the immortality of the soul to imagining it as the prolongation of life, which in turn eliminated the whole point of suffering and death. Our consent to death, she said elsewhere, was a necessary and terrible final act of obedience and should be endured in all its difficulty for precisely that reason. Death showed us that real life was elsewhere.

> The being of man is situated behind the curtain, on the supernatural side. What he can know of himself is only what is lent him by circumstances. My "I" is hidden for me (and for others); it is on the side of God; it is in God.[28]

CHRIST THE AFFLICTED ONE

Weil returned again and again to the self-emptying Christ and his affliction on the cross, accursed as a criminal and abandoned by all. This extreme of affliction was an extremity of love, the love of God. God created as an act of love and all that was created was out of love and that love extended to suffering. The extremity of this love, historically, was the accursed nature of the Cross.

> Because no other could do it, he himself went to the greatest possible distance, the infinite distance . . . this agony beyond all others, this marvel of love, is the crucifixion.[29]

Affliction, random as it was, recapitulated the distance between Father and Son in the Passion. Affliction in any person was akin to the experience of the crucifixion and was marked, above all, by distance from God, abandonment, in fact. This distance said nothing about any lack of divine providence as it was the very randomness of affliction which defined it. Suffering and affliction in people replicated the distance between Son and Father.

> (Affliction) does not mean that God's providence is lacking. It is in his providence that God has willed that necessity should be like a blind mechanism. If the mechanism were not blind there would not be any affliction. Our misery gives us the infinitely precious privilege of sharing in this distance placed

between the Son and his Father. This distance is only separation, however, for those who love.[30]

It is important that Weil's conception of affliction was of something well beyond suffering. Suffering, perhaps even "mere" suffering, was for her a natural accompaniment of a world created through the natural laws of physics with all the limitations inherent in that and in a world in which evil was at play. But affliction, an attack on the soul, was redolent of the infinite distance separating God from the creature. All that was necessary for the person in affliction, who could no longer love, was that he or she, in this affliction continued to *want* to love. The acquiescent part of the soul, even in the greatest affliction, could still be free to want to love. This wanting to love in the moment of extreme affliction placed one at the very center of the universe and, "through the thickness of the screen separating the soul from God," in the very presence of God.[31]

GRACE AS PERVASIVE

The notion of grace (a biblical term) has a checkered history in the Church and to a large extent the argument about its nature was responsible for the Reformation. Of all the views proposed during the middle ages, the one that eventually prevailed, certainly in popular religion, was that grace was a state of holiness which started with the fear of God and the need to undertake works of charity to win divine approval. Weil held that grace was the quality of God and, as such, pervaded the universe. She used the metaphor of light to describe it: Grace, as light, exposed the Truth. Grace, in Weil, was what prevailed against the counter-force of gravity and served to lift the person from the world with all its difficulties and illusions to the realm of God. It came to the person from outside. It was also associated with truth, beauty and everything which one instinctively appreciated as good.

There was a kind of bifurcation in Weil's view of the total universe—God's world and ours. There was an infinite distance in her view between God and humanity which she exemplified by a "curtain" which separated the human person from God. This curtain was pierced, albeit briefly, in those moments when, having sought God either directly or implicitly, we came to a realization of encounter with the Other. These moments of realization in an otherwise silent universe turned our mind to the basic acceptance that characterized God's reality. Although one might experience life as Void, the deeper reality was that the Void played out against a background of abiding love. Our vocation, if one can put it that way, was to wait on our raising by God, from our domain to his.

Weil's view of the reality of the universe came to affect her views on the state of humanity. Her view of her contemporaries seems to have been that people lacked, as they perhaps did not in times past, the capacity to contemplate the reality of the world of God. They had also lost sight of their own vocation to wait and listen and allow that world in. She viewed the utterly distressing reality of this world, with all its horrors and violence as reflecting the creeping rejection of God by man or perhaps man's increasing inability to wait on God in a world ever more distracting. How could it be otherwise? Against this, however, she believed with a passion in the capacity of man to leap to God as a potential within everybody. In this sense, the potential for the person to leap from the morass of the world into the arms of God was always there and always kept open because of the nature of God himself.

NOTES

1. Weil, Simone. *Oppression and Liberty.* Abingdon and New York: Routledge Classics, 2001
2. Panichas, George. *Simone Weil Reader.* Wakefield: Moyer Bell, 1977 p180
3. Panichas *Reader* p332
4. Panichas *Reader* p15
5. Panichas *Reader* p15
6. Puhl, Louis SJ. *The Spiritual Exercises of St. Ignatius.* Chicago: Loyola Press, 1952 p142–147
7. Panichas *Reader* p18
8. Panichas *Reader* p318
9. Panichas *Reader* p320
10. Weil, Simone. *Gravity and Grace.* (Crawford E and von der Ruhr M trans) London: Routledge Classics, 1999
11. Weil *Gravity and Grace* p11
12. Weil *Gravity and Grace* p15
13. Weil *Gravity and Grace* p34
14. Weil *Gravity and Grace* p82
15. Weil *Gravity and Grace* p81
16. Weil *Gravity and Grace* p84
17. Weil *Gravity and Grace* p110
18. Weil *Gravity and Grace* p112
19. Weil *Gravity and Grace* p31
20. Author's translation
21. Weil *Gravity and Grace* p35
22. Weil *Gravity and Grace* p89
23. ibid
24. Weil *Gravity and Grace* p91
25. Weil, Simone. *Waiting for God.* (Crawford E trans.) New York: Harper Perennial, 2009 p139
26. Weil, Simone *Contemplation of the Divine* in Panichas p415
27. Weil *Gravity and Grace* p33
28. Weil *Gravity and Grace* p38
29. Weil *Waiting for God* p72
30. Weil *Waiting for God* p73
31. Weil *Waiting for God* p82

Chapter Four

Spiritual Theologian

Weil's short life captures our attention on a range of issues—ethics, social order, ideology and other important issues alive in the interwar years. It is, however, in the realm of Theology that her most enduring legacy lies—a set of insights which is still being unpacked and which in many ways anticipated the core problems which theology has encountered in the second half of the twentieth century and in the unfolding of the twenty-first century. Not that Weil was in any sense systematic in her theological approach. She left no coherent treatise on understanding Christian faith. What she did leave was a rich and complex set of observations into what it means to love God and what it means that God loves us. Weil was a theologian of the Spirit and her theological legacy amounts to a challenging spirituality not quite rooted in the modern world but an appropriate response to the rootlessness of our technologically soulless society.

THEOLOGY IN THE INTERWAR YEARS: CONTEXT

Christian theology in the interwar years had encountered a number of very difficult problems. The first was its having to deal with the aftershock of Biblical criticism, essentially an endeavor of the nineteenth century. Here, European biblical scholars had recast much of the story about the origins of the Bible, both New Testament and Old, and brought the notion of revealed religion into contention. The synoptic Gospels, for example, had been shown to be, not three independent accounts of the life of Jesus happily in substantial agreement about all the essentials, but rather a set of documents which derived from the same sources but given different theological slants. The fourth gospel seemed to be an independent source but was in substantial conflict with the other three with respect to the nature of the person who was the subject of the story—Jesus. John had written not a biography but a theology where the interpretation of Jesus' mission took precedence over any real historical content. St Paul's genuine epistles were shaved to six or seven, given that most of the other, previously recognized Pauline New Testament letters had been misattributed.

The problems with the Old Testament were far worse. By the early twentieth century it was not possible to refer to the Old Testament for an account of the origins or purpose of the universe. The great dramatic acts governing the creation were reduced to colorful metaphors because science had shown that the universe had been created essentially by chance. The forming, enslavement and liberation of Israel had ceased to be history and become myth. What was able to be rescued was a narrative pointing beyond itself to the God whom Israel worshipped. History, too, had become metaphor: the substructure of the Christian religion—Old Testament as promise and New Testament as fulfillment—was, at best, an image.

If revealed religion in the interwar years was having problems, so was natural religion. Natural Theology was a sort of additional buffer to Christian theology. It derived from the belief that one could infer the existence and nature of God and the purpose of creation from nature itself. The heavens were supposed to declare the glory of God. Natural theology had an ethical concomitant too (natural ethics)—where ethical imperatives were perfectly clear from the nature of human beings themselves. However, since it was becoming apparent that God did not actively design the universe nor the world we live in, but rather, it had evolved under the forces of natural selection driven by the laws of physics, how would it be possible any longer to link the beauty of the world to the nature of God or to his intentions? God, in science, had become a redundant thesis.

A third problem faced by the theology of the interwar years was the attempt to create a form of faith which realistically accepted the limitations of Christian revelation. This was especially a problem in Protestantism where the Bible was widely viewed as the inerrant source of revelation, history and behavior. Given the progress made in biblical criticism, Theology henceforth had to operate with fewer certainties. Its task was to take seriously the fact that, in a modern world, elaborate metaphors (creation, redemption grace, trinity etc.), did not have self-evident meanings.

The notion of the possibility of faith in the interwar years was challenged by the rise of two very appealing and powerful forms of atheism—Communism and Fascism (including its most virulent form, Nazism). Both Communism and Fascism were materialist, which meant that they were, by their nature, anti-Christian. Both offered a type of counter-faith where one could lose oneself in a collective which had a higher purpose. If Christianity was a way in which the individual could form a relationship with God, these materialist ideologies engulfed the individual in a communitarian reinvention of the nature of history and the role of the person within that. Both being "scientific" in orientation, God, (being unprovable), was not part of the totalitarian package.

There were a number of theological responses to these and related challenges. Karl Barth is best remembered as a systematic theologian who drew up a vast theology on Christian dogmatics (that is, what Christians believe) while Rudolph Bultmann dealt comprehensively with the origins and makeup of the New Testament. Together with the efforts of Bernard Lonergan and Karl Rahner the work of the interwar theologians ultimately laid the basis of the work of the Second Vatican Council.

In the development of a modern theology, the basic theological questions underwent considerable evolution as one would expect from a Church trying to accommodate itself to the contemporary world as it existed rather than the world which the Church would have preferred. In Weil's France, there was a lively Catholic young workers' movement and a similar movement among students. The view of the Catholic Church was that the laity should carry out the task of changing the world in ways suggested by Catholic theology and ethics, a view built on following the publication of *Rerum Novarum* in 1891. The development of this movement of Catholic Social Action was part of the response of the Catholic Church to some of the challenges thrown up by the modern world.

WEIL'S VIEW OF THE CHURCH

Although Weil was friendly with some of the main actors in Catholic Social Action, (like Fr J-M Perrin), her religious life as a kind of proto-Catholic had very little to do with the institutional Church, an approach which was highly unusual at the time. Partly as a consequence of this, Weil's theology lacks an ecclesiology, that is, it does not situate itself within the self-understanding of the Church but was developed in a manner open to but not deriving from the Church as a community of believers. It was, in her view, the unseen recesses of other people's hearts, rather than observing the practice of Christian belief, which delivered her, as she phrased it, into the hands of Christ.[1]

Sometimes her views were hostile. She excoriated the teachings of the Council of Trent, which were, in the interwar years, the principal sources of Catholic dogma and belief. She had, she reported, nothing in common with the view of religion set forth there.[2]

In May 1942, Weil wrote a long spiritual autobiography detailing her journey in faith. It is a revealing letter in which she placed at the center her personal experience of encounter and linked it to, among other things, her reluctance to be baptized. The key reason she advanced was that the Catholic Church was not catholic enough. It excluded too much that was of value, including much that she valued and could not let go of. The God she had discovered was so much bigger than the church which claimed him. The Church's task was to be what it had the capacity to be—a community of incarnation, a bronze serpent held aloft in the desert, as she characterized it. The fact as Weil saw it, however, was that the church was a collective, suppressing the liberty which alone could allow intelligence its full potential. In her view, those who disagreed with particular dogmas of the church should be corrected but not excluded from the church nor the sacraments because, although in intellectual disagreement with the collective, they would be acting in good conscience and as a free and thinking individual. This intellectual intolerance had been, moreover, a long standing problem in Christianity. Dogma, in her view, was a matter for contemplation, a mystery which should not be unraveled. Weil pointed to the fact that, throughout history, the individual had always been something of a stranger within Christianity because he or she experienced two contradictory discourses, that which belonged within the confines of the Church and that which was constituted by prayer. The division was occasioned by the individual's intelligence over against the collective intelligence of the Church. The person discerned a difference between what was experienced in prayer and what the Church, as a collective, might be saying.

> When genuine friends of God . . . repeat words they have heard in secret amidst the silence of the union of love, and these words are in disagreement with the teachings of the Church, it is simply that the language of the market place is not that of the nuptial chamber.[3]

One can empathize, from her comments here and elsewhere, with the fact that she felt essentially unable to align herself with formal membership of the Catholic Church. The Catholic Church has many strengths but a tolerance for thinking which is not in strict agreement with the dogmatic teachings of the church has never been one of them. Certainly, in the interwar years in Europe, the Church was self-consciously a palpable, visible institution: one, holy, catholic and apostolic. Its definition of its mission was bound up with its self-perception as hierarchical, monarchical and, while inclusive of people, intolerant of theological deviation. Personal theological revelations were acceptable but only insofar as they aligned with the dogmatic stance of the church. The scope for being a Catholic while harboring and teaching divergent views was highly constrained.

The history of the modernist movement in France at the turn of the century or the fact of the later treatment of Teilhard de Chardin are both instructive.[4] It was the Church's tendency to exclude views apparently divergent from dogma which kept Weil from baptism. This was consistent with her view that the full range of intellectual positions and human experiences should be welcome within a community which described itself as catholic. Additionally, with her well-considered aversion to the collective, Weil believed that the individual could only gain any sort of authentic existence *apart from* collectives, a view consistent with her own experience.

Whether the Church actually did succeed, in the years leading up to the Second World War, in grappling with the kind of unbelief endemic to the modern world, is a moot point, especially as the conclusion of the War in 1945 was to throw up an even more complex set of problems than those confronting the Church of Weil's time. These postwar problems included the continuing progress of Communism and the pervasive loss of belief in the West.

SPIRITUALITY AND CHURCH

In retrospect, Weil's coming to a personal theology or a spirituality more or less separate from the influence of the Church as a community of believers, could be seen as part of a long tradition of people who have developed a personal relationship with the divine, even in the face of ecclesiastical opposition. Examples include John of the Cross who had to fight elements of the Church in the name of reform. Ignatius of Loyola, a further example, was a non-reader who read a book while recuperating from war wounds which began for him a long journey into a spirituality of personal transformation and service. In the mystical tradition, the person discovers God in personal direct relationship with the Other, unmediated by any mentor or community or organization. Generally, the image of the Other remains the defining bedrock over time and the perception of an original encounter continues to inform and change the person's life, possibly leading to a particular mode of service in the case of Ignatius or to a particular view of the nature of the world and the God who stands behind it in the case of Weil.

This approach to understanding faith as direct relationship is *mystical theology* and Weil was a mystical theologian. Mysticism in the Christian tradition is the experience of God as personal revelation and self communication. It is based in the experience of the radical subjectivity of the one who receives and seeks to comprehend grace. It is marked in the individual by the practice of asceticism as a response to this unique, subjective and personal revelation. Weil related how she received this personal revelation as "possession" and her writings reveal the extreme subjectivity in her interpretation of the world. Her later asceticism was of a piece with her lifelong integration of her beliefs and actions.

As we have seen, there were three encounters where Weil came in contact directly with God and received a revelation of the meaning of some of her own sufferings as redemptive. The first was in Portugal where she witnessed a procession of fishermen's wives and came to a realization of the nature of the Christian as slave. The second was in Assisi where she was drawn to prayer. The third was in Solesmes where, reciting to herself the George Herbert poem, Love, she had an experience of divine possession. There are parallels in the lives of other mystical theologians. Ignatius reported an experience at Manresa, on the banks of the Cardoner where he said that he was possessed by God in a manner similar to that which Weil reported. For one so material in his explanations, Ignatius had difficulty in elaborating on the nature of this possession but said in his autobiography that it provided the understanding and consolation he was to enjoy for the rest of his life and that nothing subsequent to that was the equal of this unsought and unmerited subjective apprehension of the presence of and acceptance by God.

FAITH AS AN EXISTENTIALIST CONSTRUCT

Faith was basic to the mystical theology of Weil and the end point of faith was authenticity—living one's life true to its potential. Faith was different from religion. Indeed, echoing an insight of Karl Barth, Weil believed that religion was generally the enemy of faith. Faith, authenticity and the distracting nature of organized religion were ideas circulating as part of the existentialist revolt of the nineteenth and twentieth centuries, a revolt which (as discussed above) began in the Lutheran Church with the writings of Søren Kierkegaard (1813–55) who was driven by the need for the individual to live his or her one life in a manner which reflected its limited duration and high potential.

It is to Kierkegaard that we owe the idea that philosophy had been asking the wrong questions—or at least an insufficient question. His writings only became accessible to European intellectual life in the early part of the twentieth century but he was to be influential in the work of most of the European philosophers in the interwar years. He held that the prime question faced by theology (and by extension, philosophy), was that of *existence*—the fact of existence rather than non-existence. Existence itself was the first datum of philosophy. The word *existential* in philosophy comes from this central concern. Our one life has to be lived by us and no-one else.

For Kierkegaard, any contemplation of one's life generated *angst* (dread). *Angst* colored everything about us and raised especially the relationship we had with a God whose existence and demands could never be proved. Living under the strain of the silence of God made authentic action difficult but necessary since we were by nature free, free to act or not to act.

There followed the next question, the individual's subjective relationship with the truth. In Kierkegaard's thinking, the fact that one's existence was limited by Death gave a definitive shape to life in the face of Death. Existence was temporal and the individual had one chance to live out the ethical. The exemplar, Abraham, was asked to sacrifice his only son and embarked on the journey to fulfill this command in obedience accompanied by *angst* at the lingering doubt that this unethical command could even come from God. In any event, Abraham attempted to follow the command but in the end was spared from carrying it through, thus being vindicated through his faith in the face of *angst*. Abraham, was prepared to abandon the thing he valued most in life (his son Isaac) in fulfillment of an unethical command of God. In rising to the test, his life was altered forever, shattered by faith in fact. In this Abraham became the Type of faith.

The person, in Kierkegaard, had to be grounded in critical self-reflection, hence his dictum "subjectivity is truth," by which he meant that the individual's subjective response to the objective in life determined a person's ethical stance. For Kierkegaard, doubt, for example, was part of faith: there was no objective certainty in religious belief: weak faith had to engender passionate commitment. These are insights common to both Kierkegaard and Weil. Faith, to be authentic, had to be a subjective relationship of complete commitment, a leap in the dark. One might argue that Kierkegaard's view, given that he was Lutheran, was a logical extension of Luther's *sola fide*. We are maintained in authentic religious belief by faith alone and certainty is error.[5]

But for Kierkegaard, faith (though it may be weak and always accompanied by the *angst* of uncertainty) was enough—enough to enable us to discern authentic action in any situation where ethical choice was at stake. Weil's model of faith was Jesus himself, the Type which could not be copied. The imitation of God required a model person to imitate and Jesus, the just man, was the one, except for the fact that at the limit One could not imitate him because the Type, the example, ended in affliction and

> one cannot choose the cross (which) is the most purely bitter suffering . . . the guarantee of its authenticity.[6]

The twentieth century European mind was to a large extent concerned with the question of how one could live one's life in a manner which had meaning through authentic choices. This helps to explain Weil, especially when we realize that this important idea, though emanating from Kierkegaard, was widespread in the theology, as well as the philosophy of the interwar years. For much of the generation writing in these years, faith and its constructive/destructive potential in the individual's life, threw up a central question for that person: his or her existence and its possibilities as the urgent question that must be resolved. Existence, that is, must be the focus of any philosophy—why existence? why *my* existence? how am I supposed to exist in the world? are there differing modes of existence mediated through choices I make? This new theme, basic to twentieth century European philosophy, that the fact of existence itself was the prime datum of philosophical endeavor, also became central to Weil's stark theology.

Fundamental to this philosophy in both its religious and non-religious form, was the notion of the leap of faith. Faith was conceived as akin to falling in love: one did not embark on it for reasons of objective judgment and it involved an admixture of doubt. Despite doubt, one leapt into faith and took the consequences. One had no proof of God, for example, but one took the journey of faith anyway, carrying one's doubts with one. To do otherwise was not faith but mere credulity. Christian faith, in the existentialist view, rode on a bedrock of doubt. As far as Christian beliefs and doctrines were concerned, one could not know the extent to which any of them was true, but the believer committed to them anyway because it was the relationship of absolute commitment which defined authentic faith. Weil pushed this existentialist insight further. God was encountered in the middle of the Void that constituted one's life. That Void was where the grace of God was too because grace filled up the empty spaces. By analogy, the soul needed to acknowledge a void within to receive grace. It followed that, for each person, the Void, where it was not already perceived, had to be created.[7]

The widespread existentialist view of faith as a leap into encounter had many proponents in the twentieth century. Even among post-Christian philosophers there developed a related view, that action in the world created meaning. It was an attractive idea, first because there was resonance with the image of the individual's having to make a choice in sympathy with the realization of his or her own existence and the potential for action in accord with the fundamental meaning of life. Secondly, there was widespread acceptance of the idea that proper action might be accompanied by feelings of *angst* and that the individual faced a choice between authentic and inauthentic existence. This choice was captured by the metaphor of the leap into darkness.

One continuing outcome of this approach, especially in the years around the Second World War, was the potent idea that action in a world of conflicting values created meaning for the individual. Weil did not subscribe to this view because in her view faith should lead to the search for God involving a *kenosis*, or emptying of the personal aspects of the self with a view to allowing space for encounter, this encounter pointing the individual towards Truth. She did, however, hold to the view that *kenosis* constituted action, indeed the most potent action we were able to undertake.

Quite apart from the fact that Weil explored much of the same existentialist territory, albeit with a different language, her theological writings clearly picked up and reflected Kierkegaard's initial insight and reprised his view that the bourgeois nature of the modern Church had stifled the passion which should characterize faith. In Kierkegaard, religious observance had nothing to do with faith because it did not involve a personal confrontation with God.

As in the case of Abraham, faith was encounter. Faith, if embraced, was passion. Faith engendered *angst*. Faith was a leap beyond rationality into the unknown. And, of course, faith was lonely. Kierkegaard's insights on faith are therefore sometimes echoed, or rediscovered in the writings of Weil. Faith, as with Abraham, was also a relationship: but as she said, it was not simple consolation. God did not bring comfort and protection for the soul as a reward for faith. On the contrary, if we wanted to find protection, consolation and reward, we would need to love something other than God.[8]

Faith, in Christianity, as Weil saw it, was *kenotic*; its hallmark was self-emptying as in the example of Christ. She focused on the self emptying of Christ which St. Paul referred to and extended it to the individual. The individual was called to do just that: empty self of everything which was not grace, even the desire for grace and to fix the will on the Void because the good which the person sought, being undefinable, was part of the Void. This self emptying focus on the Void was at the heart of Weil's spirituality. Once the Void is acknowledged in the individual, the person is open to having it filled—by God.[9]

Faith was also, in Weil, characterized by prayer. Prayer, as we have seen, was a mark of this total reliance on God. It was a relationship with God marked by *attendance*, literally attendance or being present to the other. It meant the one-to-one communication between two differing personalities. This relationship continued whether the other was present or not. Being there and focusing on the Other was the heart of prayer and prayer was the acknowledgement of faith.

A MYSTICISM WITHOUT ILLUSION

Weil as mystic understood and even embraced the world in which she was living. An intriguing fact, as far as her life as a mystic went, was that she was without illusion as to the nature of human existence. In her university days, in Paris in the interwar years, Weil immersed herself in the writings of Marx among others and was attracted by the concept of the operation of an historical dialectic. But she came to the conclusion that the professional revolutionary set which Marx had spawned was immersed in illusions about the real state of human nature and especially the tendency of the human ego to undermine any collective effort. Nor did Weil place any trust in the outcomes of a power shift from the dominant to the victimized. She viewed the modern person as largely alone with the historical networks of culture and social order fractured. This rootlessness, as she called it, was reflected in but not confined to the soulless nature of capitalist factory work. Rootless man was vulnerable to the modern state, both in its blandishments and in its demand for compliance. Weil outlined her views in *The Need for Roots*.[10] In it she called for a new commitment to the noble practice of politics—to overcome chauvinism, militarism and alienation. But at the time, social man, as such, was seen as essentially rootless and lost in a mass culture which neutered the potential for self-transcendence.

This view of modern, western man as essentially lost in a mass culture of alienation, fractured community and crumbling personal relations was not confined to Weil. It was shared by other philosophers at the time and afterwards, Martin Heidegger for example. Heidegger (1889–1976) flourished in the interwar years as the exponent of a philosophy of being and built his analysis on the disjunction between the real and the apparent. In Heidegger's case, unfortunately, his cultural pessimism went the opposite way from Weil's, towards Nazism.

Modern western man, this person who was the subject of so much European interwar philosophy, was lost in social alienation. Nevertheless, in Weil, he or she could set out on a road to discover God (even if the person were an atheist, God having both an impersonal and a personal aspect) and could form a relationship through prayer.

ATHEISM

Weil said that she began life as an atheist although today she would probably be characterized as agnostic. Atheism was, as it is today, the default stance of the intellectual. Her view was that this could be a starting stage on the road to faith. Indeed, for Weil, atheism was both respectable and if genuinely held, superior to much of the practice of religion. She played with the notion that there were two atheisms, one of which involved a purification of the notion of God, a refining of the person's imagination to eliminate the accretions of self consolation which crept into people's ideas about what they would like God to be. True faith, she said, involved nothing to do with consolation and to the extent that religion taught the consolations of belief it was a hindrance to true faith. It followed that the person needed to have an atheistic component in his or her makeup: the part of the person not made for God.[11]

But all people must beware that they must find God, by whatever name they call him in the impersonal because God's own perfection is the quintessence of the impersonal. "Every atheist is an idolater—unless he is worshipping the true God in his impersonal aspect."[12]

Moreover, by conforming our selves to the impersonal aspect of God, we exhibit love of God, irrespective of whether we believe or not and God and to this person God will manifest his existence.[13]

Weil's atheism was to some extent natural to the person and, unlike the theologian grounded in the Church, she did not seek to convert, only to describe.

> It is not for man to seek or even to believe in God. He has only to refuse his love to everything which is not God. This refusal does not presuppose any belief. It is enough to recognize what is obvious to any mind, that all the goods of this world are limited and radically incapable of satisfying the desire which burns perpetually within us for an infinite and perfect good. . . . If one persists indefinitely in refusing to devote the whole of one's love to things unworthy of it, which means everything in this world without exception, that is enough. . . . A man has only to persist in this refusal and one day or another God will come to him. He will see and hear and cling to God. . . . For any man of whom God has taken possession the doubt concerning the reality of God is purely abstract.[14]

For most mystical theologians, the journey of the soul begins somewhere after the person has become a believing and praying person. For Weil, the journey of the soul began in the heart of the atheistic and material world, where the thought of belief and commitment to the grace of God was absent and where the individual had, at best, an inchoate appreciation of the existence of a supernatural world and the possibility of an invitation to be part of it. Natural atheism was part of taking the world for what it was and accepting the fact that the first inclination of the human person was to try to escape the suffering which characterized the world or, failing that, to understand it. Initial atheism was a natural accompaniment to this stage of the person's existence. The first step in reaching beyond that was to recognize that one had an existence as a soul, that the soul sensed that it lived in a Void and that that Void needed to be accepted. The Void in Weil's view was both a diminution in the person and an opportunity, for without the realization of the Void, there would be no opportunity for God to enter and occupy it, in somewhat the same fashion as a gas enters and occupies a partial vacuum.

> Our life is nothing but impossible absurdity. Each thing that we desire is in contradiction with the conditions . . . attaching to that thing: each assertion that we make implies the contrary assertion: all our feelings are mixed up with their opposites. . . . Contradiction alone makes us experience the fact that we are not All. Contradiction is our wretchedness and the feeling of our wretchedness is the feeling of reality. Our wretchedness is not something we concoct. It is something truly real. That is why we must love it.[15]

For Weil, the encounter of the soul with God, if it happened at all, took place in the Void—the empty part of oneself where we lacked everything we felt we truly needed. If the encounter happened, it happened suddenly as in a lightning flash. We have all experienced, she believed, these flashes of insight where contemplation or intuition or even brushes with the Void carry us for a moment into the realm of the supernatural.[16] Prayer is at the heart of mystical theology. It is the direct awareness, to the point of possession, of the Other, the Beloved. The response to this possession by the Other is prayer, which, for Weil was encounter, silence, waiting and desire. She held that we must consent to the inroads of the Other. Prayer as this consent to desire is often confused in Catholic theology with mere petition, but for Weil its simplicity was crucial. The attention which constituted prayer was actually desire and properly considered, prayer was not an act of the will but an expression of desire for the Other, a consent to be in relationship. The fulfillment of this desire or consent was a slow disappearance of the personal, the ego, and a slow conformity to the impersonal nature of God.[17] Prayer in Weil's writing was really a substitute for much that would constitute a theology in other writers. Despite her deep formation in philosophy, she avoided developing anything that looked like a theology for the 20th century. Notwithstanding the lack of a formal structure, there was an analog to her approach in St Paul, who put as central to his theology both the person of Jesus and his self-emptying sacrifice on the one hand and the redemptive role of the Cross on the other.

In Weil's theology, prayer was attending to the Other, attention that was absolute. Once the person had within him or herself the spark of a relationship with the divine, then nothing really remained to be done save to care for it and allow it to flourish. Her own experience was the discovery of prayer as attention in her moment of "possession" after which she carried the memory as just such a dynamically remembered moment of engagement. Weil reported that, when working on Thibon's farm prior to departing for the US, she recited the Lord's prayer with particular attention to the meaning of the words, repeating the exercise in the case of any memory lapse. We cannot dissociate this view from her intense focus in all relationships on active listening and clear communication, attention being something that one owed everyone one met. Prayer, for Weil was attention because it was the medium of a relationship, any relationship actually, though in prayer a relationship that had two disparate sides, the divine and the human, conducted across a Void where one had to struggle for the power to listen to the meaningful silence of God.

One of the astonishing facets of Weil's theology is the thoroughness and speed with which she grasped the meaning of the heart of Christian theology. She referred constantly to the Gospels and, as a classical scholar, it is reasonable to assume that she understood them thoroughly through reading them in the Greek originals. But Weil's actual theology was redolent of St Paul whose interest was not so much the life of Jesus as the significance of it and of the Cross which defined it. Her theological categories were the self-emptying of Jesus, the sufferings of the Cross, the voluntary nature of that suffering, the relationship of Jesus with the Father and the affliction which characterized his life. It was in her consideration of affliction that her theology and the vector of her life coincided.

AT THE HEART OF HER THEOLOGY: AFFLICTION

Weil linked suffering, which was at the base of her understanding of prayer, to her idea of decreation. Decreation can be connected in Weil to St Paul's notion of Christ's self-emptying. In the letter to the Philippians, Paul pointed out that Christ emptied himself in becoming human and then emptied himself again by dying the death of a slave. This emptying of self, or *kenosis*, Weil saw as an act of supreme love and the cosmic model of love. Emulating this act of love pointed to the need for *kenosis* in ourselves and the first step was to begin the task of reducing the personal in ourselves to allow the impersonal wider scope—decreation. Decreation of part of ourselves was necessary in order that there could be a proper space between man and God. This necessity created a distance, setting up a tension or a space within which we could surrender to the approach from God. This distance-to-allow-love also determined much of the nature of the world in which the soul found itself, that is to say, the Void which we have seen was her starting point. In Weil, the wretchedness of the world, all its distress, poverty and suffering were elements of the love of God because they were a natural consequence of God's withdrawal from us and the world to allow the person to be. Only distance between the person and God could allow this relationship, this love, to exist in the first place. The only thing we had in forming a relationship with the Other was our selves, our "I". This element of the ego which each of us had was there to be surrendered. Without the obvious distance between ourselves and God, without the screen as she termed it, we could not exist in the first place. Surrendering the ego in ourselves meant recognizing the need for this screen and pushing through it. It was for the individual to pierce through the screen so that the ego of the person ceased to be.[18]

Affliction (*malheur*) followed. The affliction of the world was what alerted us to the fact that we were living in our own temporal world, not some paradise. It brought into reality that which we might otherwise have thought impossible. Both suffering and affliction were constitutive of the nature of the person, just part of reality. Moreover, it was just as constitutive of our nature to flee from suffering and fly to pleasure, which was why we naturally associated joy with the good and suffering with evil. But as we have seen, in Weil's theology, suffering was not evil: it was potentially redemptive. Pleasure and pain were companions and the more we appreciated joy in life, the more intense would be its loss, that is, suffering. This intensification of suffering enlarged our capacity to feel compassion for others. Suffering is related to joy in the same manner as hunger is to food.[19]

Weil wrote that affliction, which was beyond suffering and which was at the heart of her spirituality, was not an unfortunate byproduct of the nature of reality. It was part of the existential makeup of the human soul. The human soul, in Weil's view, was vulnerable, threatened by malign forces on all sides. This was most evident, in the world in which we live, in the form of the slave who was nothing in the eyes of the owner and eventually became nothing in his own eyes. This power over the soul turned the active subject into an acted-upon object of others. It was utterly disempowering and literally soul-destroying, especially given the arbitrary origins of such affliction. But affliction demonstrated to us that we were not living in paradise and, in its absence, we would just settle for the good as nothing but an absence of pain.

The ultimate victim of affliction was Christ, who, being master of Truth, did not waver in his faith in the Father through all his sufferings, innocent and victim as he was. Christ's emptiness met the fullness of the Father in the Cross and its aftermath. He embraced the emptiness and suffering of the cross and established the definitive shape and content of human authenticity.

Affliction could be the result of harm done to us, for all of us from time to time have been victims of another's malice. If this damage done to us were such as to reach the depth of our soul we would face a decision about affliction and consequent revenge.

Revenge might reduce the level of affliction experienced by the soul by passing some of the hurt onto the other person. The course of revenge, however, would do nothing to reduce the harm of the offense: in fact it would increase it. Accepting the harm and internalizing it, to some degree emptying oneself in accepting the injustice imposed and the resulting hurt, would serve to stop the spread and increase of harm and limits it for other people. We would be free to choose to accept and therefore limit suffering or to convert it into a multiplication of suffering for others to endure.

EVIL

The problem of God, if one can put it that way, and therefore the problem of prayer for most people, is generally related to the problem of evil, that is to say, how can I relate to a God who permits evil? This is also problematic for the consideration of prayer. If one cannot get past the problem of evil how could one get to the point of prayer? It bears repeating that Weil responded to this in her basic view on the necessity of evil as part of God's withdrawal to allow humans to be humans. She extended the tension in the problem of evil even further in her discussion of the affliction which lay beyond suffering. Suffering, in itself was not surprising. Still less did it bring into question either the existence or the nature of God. Given that God had withdrawn from the world to allow the person to be, the necessary adjunct to his non presence was evil and the world was full of criminal types prepared to persecute the innocent. As for disease and the wasting of the body, these were the unavoidable consequences of the play of the laws of the universe and, given the nature of matter, life could not have been otherwise. But what she found surprising was what lay beyond suffering, that is affliction, which destroyed the soul, including the souls of the innocent.

> But it *is* surprising that God should have given affliction the power to seize the very souls of the innocent and to take possession of them as their sovereign lord. At the very best, he who is branded by affliction will keep only half his soul.[20]

For Weil, the afflicted one, being at the outer edge of human responsiveness, did not attract human compassion, rather as Christ in dereliction on the Cross did not. In the extreme of affliction (and her model here was the plight of the slave) there was nothing left to love. The soul might therefore actually cease to love, meaning that God became utterly absent. The soul, however, had the capacity either to love in emptiness or to desire to love. This faint trace of connection with the divine, this desire to love again, would be enough and in the fullness of time would reveal itself as actually a relationship with the Other. Desire was prayer: desire was relationship.

Weil's reflections on affliction and its role in establishing in our minds the true nature of human personality were extensive and it is clear that she was speaking from subjective experience. The point of these reflections in her writings was to assert the model of Christ as the Afflicted One. Put another way, her notion of affliction drew to some extent on her experiences on the factory floor where she encountered the worker as devoid of choice. This lack of choice, she believed, was the mark of the slave with affliction being a characteristic of slavery. Affliction was beyond pain and had both a physical and a psychological aspect. There was no cure save to continue to persevere in love. The suffering person, at the extreme, suffered the dislocation from community that constituted affliction. Affliction was pain but more than that. It was alienation from other people who might otherwise have understood and supported. The person was alone in a situation in which he was innocent, thus deepening his estrangement and the impotency he confronted. All this was like slavery and the afflicted was the slave. Christ was the definitively afflicted one. Christ was the slave. His only response was to persist in love.

CONTRADICTION

Weil's spirituality found its roots in her conception of the standing of the person within the universe. In her view, the pursuit of the good enmeshed people in a tangle of contradictions whereby what they desired was contradicted by the consequences. For example, improving people's standard of living endangered their soul. For Weil, this set of contradictions at the center of our lives had to be accepted because there was no alternative. The contradictions which tore at us reflected something of the nature of God. Gustave Thibon, commenting on Weil's view, pointed out that for those who wanted only goodness, this notion stood in the way of the obvious nexus between good and evil. Good was to evil as light to shadow, a universal law that, if not recognized, could lead to affliction.[21] For Weil, purity of heart for those seeking a way through the contradictions of life only served to deepen suffering while giving it a meaning. The glory of Christianity, she held, was that it did not seek to deny suffering nor to find a supernatural cure for it, but to discern a supernatural use for it.[22]

Weil saw the Incarnation as the absolute expression of the function of Christ, the self-emptying of God, his reduction to the lowest form of humanity (afflicted slave)—God assuming the condition of the creature to show us the path to undoing the ego or gravity in ourselves.[23]

SIMONE WEIL'S THEOLOGY TODAY AND HER SPIRITUAL LEGACY

Weil was the eternal outsider and her inspiration was the life of Jesus and its meaning, a life of poverty, a life of self-giving, a life of servant-leadership and prayer. She strove in her living to imitate Jesus who emptied himself not only in his incarnation but also in the pattern of his daily life. Her quest was ever closer union with him and ever more authentic identification with him in his abandonment, suffering and rejection. Despite Weil's extreme intellectualism, she fought to keep her spirituality free from any intellectual framework. Her mode was rather contemplation and ascent to wonder which, in turn, demanded attentiveness. This attention presupposed faith, even the faith that came briefly like a lightning flash. It also implied love because the waiting was about desire. Total attention, whether to God or another person in need was, in her view, prayer.[24]

What are we to make of the mystical experiences in Weil's life and the theology implicit in her enigmatic and complex metaphors?

In the final analysis we are dealing with a spirituality rather than simply a theology. That is to say, we are dealing with the *reportage* of a soul who was surprised by an encounter with God. This was not a soul who had set out on a long journey of discovery and been rewarded by a vision of the Other—as, for example in the case of Ignatius. This was someone who had come up in life through an intellectual set of constructs which were materialist and socially reformist. She even retained some regard for Marx to the end.

Weil's experience of possession took her unawares and challenged her accustomed ways of thinking, the comforting communitarian nostrums of the Left. Of course, she was open to possession by the Other, being one of those whom she described as loving God in his impersonal aspect, but the moment of divine possession itself was unexpected and an undeniable disjunction with her past.

In Weil, we are dealing with a soul who lived in an intellectual world of pervasive atheism. The natural vector for the development of her disruptive vision, the Church, was widely regarded as powerful, institutionally indolent and, to a significant extent, corrupt. Indeed, that was how she regarded it. Other mystics had to battle for their vision against the flow of an uncomprehending Church. John of the Cross was imprisoned; Ignatius was for a time in the hands of the Inquisition; Joan of Arc was burnt at the stake for her visions. But Weil never resiled one iota from her view of the Church as a disappointment: an authentic community of the Cross to be sure, but comprehensively failing at every challenge nevertheless. Even today, her reputation within the Church is ambiguous: was she heterodox opponent or critical defender of the Church? A less ambiguous role might have allowed Weil's spirituality to have had wider influence within the Church. Just as Kierkegaard remained a disturbing outsider in the Church because he never accommodated himself to any of its structures, so Weil remained the eternal outsider within the Church to which she belonged, hanging on in the ecclesiastical consciousness as the Catholic family's black sheep. Weil's mystical journey was simultaneously recognizable as Catholic and at the same time not.

The consequence of what Weil saw as her encounter with God was that she endured a loneliness of uncompromising commitment to the logic of the Cross. The life she followed, after her mystical encounters, became one of suffering, alienation, affliction, the incomprehension of others and the constant struggle to define the point of it all—the point, that is, of redemption. Weil did not lock herself up in a convent to contemplate the divine. She remained in a world she understood as lost, depraved, empty, and, for most, a struggle where wresting any meaning was on the verge of impossible. Yet it was precisely here on the limit where abandonment glimpsed the possibility of Love, that Weil saw that God took his stance. She continued to work for struggling people and for the soul of France in that most difficult of ages in the only way she could, given her limitations, by dialogue, by exposition and by logic. Had Weil been more personable, she might have had a wider audience in the last years of her life. All we have now are her words, texts never meant for publication, and these are unmediated by our knowing her, the woman. The text we have reflects an uncompromising exposition of the logic, for today and always, of the Cross of Christ and its implications for anyone who wants to follow in simple footsteps the way of Jesus. Weil provided no comfort: the way she laid out was difficult and could bring suffering to the point of self-annihilating affliction.

Although Weil did not write theology in any formal sense, in assessing her for today we can see that her spirituality was formed around faith, as any must be. She saw the journey of faith as a response to an opportunity which God offered to all. For Weil, the *opportunity* to know God was pervasive but the soul must assent and then subject itself to the loneliness that would come with human freedom. God progressed to the soul but the soul must make a cognate journey to God. The difficulty of this journey was the soul's cross. Moreover, faith must make the journey through the silence of God. What faith required was a brief moment of consent, even if surrendered reluctantly. That moment was the instant when God took possession of the soul. But in Weil's theology, it was God's will that we live, that we be, that we work out our existential potential within a world that could not be otherwise. At the moment of possession, therefore God abandoned the soul, withdrew to allow it to grope towards him through all the detritus and sufferings of life, across the impossible obstacles of space and time. The soul's personal pilgrimage was to grope in search of the One it loved and to meet somewhere at the end of the journey the God who had made the same journey from the other end. That challenge, realizing it and undertaking it was actually what constituted the cross.[25]

A PERSON FOR TODAY

We live in an age of universal skepticism. There is a widespread skepticism of the traditional institutions of our societies. Looking at these institutions, there is hardly one which is not the subject of cynicism. The armed forces, the police forces, the judiciary, young people's clubs, political structures and parties and educational institutions all operate in an environment of widespread distrust and amid calls for greater transparency and accountability. The Church is one such institution and it suffers more than most from this social cynicism. It is not a promising environment for faith to be encountered.

Moreover, there has been a cultural drift from the natural respect afforded the Church because there has been a drift from widespread acceptance of the existence and call of God. The Church and what it offers only make sense to those who accept the reality of a God. In the West, this drift has been accentuated by the high living standards we have come to expect since the Second World War. A high degree of social security may not normally make for a heightened dependency on God, such is the common notion of providence. Perhaps it should not either.

Nor does contemporary culture interpret positively the notion of the silence of God. In Karl Barth's terms, we have no propensity for allowing God to be God. If God exists why does he not patently manifest himself and be done with it—the kind of no-nonsense approach our culture takes to all important political and social questions.

Neither does our society accommodate death well and it makes no attempt to integrate any significance death might have into the understanding of life and its possible meanings. We tend to be, by contrast, a death-denying culture. Death has no meaning because life itself, the universe, the cosmos have no meaning save that which we might like to invest in it individually as we see fit.

The life and spirituality of Weil are well suited to addressing the issue of the possibility of Faith in this fractured cultural environment.

First, hers was a type of faith possibility which was quite independent of natural theology. She knew that the chance creation of the universe and all within it did not mean that it had left us empty of God. Although God was quite separate from creation, creation itself was the surface upon which the encounter with God was a possibility, a possibility offered to everyone. The proof of the existence and action of God were to be found in the contemplation of the meaning of our own existence. In that sense the discovery of God was, in principle, open to all.

Secondly, Weil's notion of Christian faith did not necessitate Church. The Church, in her view was always a scandal of some sort but it was the medium by which the account of Jesus and his life and relationship with the Father was passed on. But it was not strictly necessary to be integrated into the Church to grasp its faith. The Church was needed because it was one of the institutions which anchored people to a community and a culture and these in turn were the factors which opened us to the supernatural, together with literature and the other artifacts of culture.

Thirdly, Weil's view of faith started with the observation that there was nothing inherently incompatible in atheism. Indeed, she saw it, properly understood, as a starting point of faith. For her, faith was an individual experience which began in all who possessed it as an initiative of God. What was required was response and the possibility of response remained open to all at all times. Faith could be mistaken for the routine responses, habits and customs which the Church offered but the personal knowledge of God was possible for all and that was a mark of divine mercy. Consolation in religion was a danger because it was false: "Religion, insofar as it is a source of consolation," as she put it, "is a hindrance to true faith; and in this sense atheism is purification."[26]

Fourthly, Faith was always on offer till the point of acceptance by the individual. As long as the person were alive, the possibility remained of an encounter with God. Moreover, the person might reprise in later life an interrupted journey long abandoned. Faith as encounter invited the journey.

Fifthly, we come to the question of how this view of faith might affect the issue of authenticity in people's lives, an issue which Weil touched on implicitly. Authenticity is not a word in common use, but the ideal which lies behind it is still abroad. Most people, especially younger people, want to live a life that has meaning and they are often prepared to challenge the cultural and consumer emptiness of much of modern life to reach for that. Weil's spirituality provides a way of acknowledging and embracing the harsh realities of life, at the same time as laying out a path through them. The world can indeed be grasped as a Void, a feeling we might comprehend existentially. But this Void is necessary because it generates our need of God. Evil, being part of this Void is inevitable. Authenticity requires enduring the Void and ultimately accepting death as part of the meaning of life. Taking the risk of enduring the Void is authentic life. But we can learn to love ourselves and each other in all this because of the love of God for us.

The problem of evil, the question of purpose in life, the real nature of sin ("nothing else but the failure to recognize human wretchedness"), the emptying of the self, the acceptance of suffering (or beyond that, affliction) as a source of knowledge; these and other reflections bear on the nature of the questioning about the modern world, at least for those people actually asking the questions. All these and more Weil encompassed in her spirituality.

An examination of Weil's spirituality needs, at some point, to determine where it fits with the notion of church. After all, Christian spirituality is derived from Christ and our knowledge of Christ comes through a continuing Christian community. Weil was distrustful of all forms of collective as they tended to dilute the individual's desire for the truth an observation she would repeat in her call for the abolition of all political parties. For her, all social order (all political arrangements designed to order the lives of people) was open to doing evil. It was plain in scripture that the world was unavoidably under the domination of the prince of this world, the one who tempted Jesus in the gospel by offering it to him. All one could do in this circumstance was to try to limit the evil which any collective would spawn. As for the Church as a collective, and given its propensity to self worship, it was probably more dangerous on account of the good which it contained than on account of the evil which undermined it.[27]

Weil's view of the Church was not so much hostile as dialectical, that is, she affirmed and she denied. She affirmed that the church existed for all and that its central beliefs were compatible with other apparently alien religious traditions. This meant in turn that the boundaries of the church were wider than the church realized, especially as the Roman church still bore so many of the characteristics of the Roman Empire which, for her, was the quintessence of force. Weil's distrust of patriotism was of a piece with her distrust of all loyalties here below on Earth which fell short of a universal loyalty to, and compassion for, humanity. In other words, Weil thought the Catholic Church should be more catholic. Writing to Fr. Perrin of her status as a Christian she said

> Christianity should contain all vocations without exception since it is catholic. In consequence, the Church should also. But in my eyes Christianity is catholic by right but not in fact. So many things are outside it, so many things that I love and do not want to give up, so many things that God loves otherwise they would not be in existence.[28]

Weil believed that this search for a truly inclusive Christian collective had a particular urgency at that moment in history. Its challenge was to show the world what a truly incarnated Christianity looked like. Doubtless she had in mind the potential for demonstrating the opportunities for compassion and the uses of suffering to a world weighed down by the War and the manifold horrors which accompanied it. Weil admitted that the church had to have boundaries and to exist as a social structure but, given that all structures were "irreducibly that of the prince of this world," she posited the dialectic of the good (the life of Christ, the gospel) and the countervailing evil (the structure). The tendency within any structure, including the Roman church was to self-worship. This self-worship was a kind of patriotism which must dilute the Church's necessary commitment to all humanity. In it, the message was overwhelmed by the structure, the church being worshipped instead of Christ, the machine becoming more important than the Incarnation it existed to proclaim.

Weil's insight was that the Church was summoned to self-transcendence, to become that which it was not, to rise above the patriotism inherent in all social structures and to allow the Incarnation to be incarnate in its own structure. In this she was prescient. The problems that Weil recognized as her own have become the problems of the Church itself, especially the problems that have derived from an overwhelming emphasis on the reputation and strength of the Church as opposed to the integrity of its witness and message. Again to Perrin, Weil wrote

> We have to be catholic, that is to say, not bound by so much as a thread to any created thing, unless it be to creation in its totality. . . . It is true that we have to love our neighbor, but, in the example that Christ gave as an illustration of this commandment, the neighbor is a being of whom nothing is known, lying naked, bleeding and unconscious on the road. It is a question of completely anonymous, and for that reason, completely universal love. . . . Today, it is not nearly enough to be a saint, but we must have the saintliness demanded of the present moment.[29]

Weil's true spirituality was as much in evidence in the life she led as in the words she wrote. Weil said that she came to faith not through the medium of the church but through the grace of Christ, by direct and unsought possession. The life she lived subsequently was one of critical analysis of herself in relationship to God and to others, and of a continued meditation on the nature of social structures and what constituted authentic social action. Because she was no mere theoretician, there seems in her life little contradiction between her spiritual journey and her writings. The elaborate analogs which Weil deployed in describing the encounter of the soul with the world and with God, seemed fully constitutive of her own direct sufferings: void, detachment, renunciation, decreation, affliction and so on. All these and other categories seemed directly drawn from the life she lived and to have been wrung out of her through painful experience.

Finally, concerning Weil's mysticism and from the vantage point of today, one needs to recognize that it is a stumbling block to her supporters. Although mysticism is well understood in Catholic experience, Weil's approach to describing it was somewhat oblique. Robert Coles pointed to a Protestant edge to it.

> With that escalation of her thought into the realm of religious faith . . . she would lose the assent, maybe even the interest, of many intellectuals who otherwise found her writing provocative, if not congenial.
>
> She had quite obviously been yearning for even more than such a contemplation of divinity: she craved an ultimate or transcendent conversation with God. This kind of faith—an existentialism of a rather special and demanding kind—puts her in the company of Kierkegaard rather than Pascal: a Protestant rather than a Catholic existentialism.[30]

Weil's transcendent universalism and rootedness in the modern world perhaps explain much of her spiritual attraction and her highly specialized appeal. We do not expect the church to have the language, the experience, nor the sympathy to speak with much conviction to the modern world. It might well fracture if it did. But in Weil we do have one example of a contemporary mysticism which goes to the heart of modernity and, whether it quite coheres entirely with our historic understanding of dogma, it certainly coheres with the inner core of the gospel itself.

NOTES

1. Letter to J-M Perrin 26 May 1942
2. Letter 1951
3. Panichas, George. *Simone Weil Reader*. Wakefield: Moyer Bell, 1977 p23
4. Pius X issued a number of encyclicals against modernism, a movement within the Catholic Church aimed at promoting biblical criticism. One of the targets of the anti-modernist movement was the role of private speculation in a manner contrary to the dogmatic definitions of the Church.In 1950, Teilhard de Chardin, Jesuit palaeontologist, was admitted to the French Academy of Science, but in 1957 Teilhard's works were banned by the Holy Office.
5. Martin Luther took the view that the individual was put in a right relationship with God ("justified") not through the good works which he performed and which demonstrated that he was a charitable person, but solely through faith, by which he meant complete reliance on and

dependence on God. *Sola fide* (by faith alone) became a catch cry of the Protestant Reformation.

    6. Weil, Simone. *Gravity and Grace.* (Crawford E and von der Ruhr M *trans*) London: Routledge Classics, 1999 p88

    7. Weil *Gravity and Grace* p10–11
    8. Weil *Gravity and Grace*
    9. Weil *Gravity and Grace*
    10. Weil, Simone. *The Need for Roots.* London and New York: Routledge Classics, 2002
    11. Weil *Gravity and Grace* p115
    12. Last Notebook (1942) p308
    13. Weil *Gravity and Grace*—Detachment p12
    14. Weil, Simone. *Gateway to God.* (David Raper ed.) Glasgow: Collins, 1974 p85
    15. Weil *Gateway* p63
    16. Weil *Gravity and Grace* p11
    17. Weil *Gravity and Grace* p15
    18. Weil *Gravity and Grace* p32
    19. Weil *Gravity and Grace* p83–4
    20. Weil, Simone. *Waiting for God.* (Crawford E *trans*.) New York: Harper Perennial, 2009 p69
    21. Weil *Gravity and Grace,* Introduction pxxvii
    22. ibid
    23. ibid
    24. Weil *Gravity and Grace* p116
    25. Weil S. *Gravity and Grace* p88
    26. Wills, Arthur (trans). *The Notebooks of Simone Weil.* London: Routledge and Keegan Paul 1956 p220
    27. Weil *Gravity and Grace* p166
    28. Panichas *Reader* p20
    29. Panichas *Reader* p114
    30. Coles, Robert. *Simone Weil: a modern pilgrimage.* Woodstock: SkyLight Paths Publishing, 2001 p151

Chapter Five

Politics and the Possible

SIMONE WEIL'S LAST WORK — THE NEED FOR ROOTS

The last six years of Weil's life produced, though in unpublished form, a large and important set of writings on theology and spirituality and quite distinct from her previous work, on different aspects of politics. In the final year of her life Weil was engaged by the Free French, at her request, to address the question of the nature of France and the type of society which might emerge once France was liberated. This was to be an exercise in practical politics, or as one would call it today, public policy. The study which she produced, however, ended up more as reflection on the human condition than a practical report to assist French reconstruction. T.S Eliot described the resulting work, *The Need for Roots*, as "prolegomena" to politics, that is, a work which precedes particular political arguments, but which serves as a general background to the consideration of a particular politics. Weil's views were drawn from French culture but ultimately claimed universal application. She wrote it as part of her work for the Free French while in London and although her conception of the faults of France and their remedy were disregarded at the time, it remains important in any reflection on the nature of her approach to politics and culture.

Much of the argument in *The Need for Roots* was a dialogue between Weil's view of history and her view of the human condition, with one interpreting the other. As far as she was concerned, the most recent evidence for the pervasive uprootedness in France was its fall to German forces in 1940. That fall had been characterized by widespread inertia and alienation among the people, including the industrial workforce. For Weil, Vichy and Petain were simply symbols of France's desire to go on sleeping in the stupor generated by the type of life France had lived in the first half of the twentieth century. Although *The Need for Roots* was aimed at a better and more integrated political culture, it was grounded in the recent experience of France.

> The French people in June and July 1940 were not a people waylaid by a band of ruffians, whose country was suddenly snatched from them. They are a people who opened their hands and allowed their country to fall to the ground. Later on—but after a long interval—they spent themselves in ever more and more desperate efforts to pick it up again: but someone had placed his foot upon it.[1]

The source of the languid approach by the French to their own freedom was, in Weil's eyes, their lack of *rootedness* and the intrusion of alienation into all aspects of French life. France had been shamed by its loss to Hitler's armies and by the compromises which had followed the capitulation. One of the chief sources of this failure had been the political system which the Third Republic had spawned and the interplay of political parties which had flourished under it.

From Weil's perspective, the shame of the French Republic was collective and personal. Every French person had some role and some cause for shame. She was adamant that the French should not forget or minimize the importance of the disaster which had overtaken them. To give way to such a temptation, she believed, would be to ruin the collective soul of the country.[2]

In 1940–2, after the occupation, there was widespread support in France for the Vichy government. Although there was a resistance movement during those early years of the War, it was not widely supported and was not as extensive as subsequent mythology suggests. French structures like the police found themselves at the service of the occupying Germans and not always reluctantly so. France's colonies largely remained strong supporters of Petain with Vichy continuing to carry on the War against the allies. Allied and French forces still under French control clashed in battle occasionally, including at sea. French colonial resistance to the Allies continued in North Africa up to the end of 1942 and in the Far East until the end of the War. French authorities were fully complicit in the transportation of 72,000 Jews to death camps both within and outside Vichy. The *maquis*, a vicious paramilitary police force within Vichy controlled areas, was emblematic of French double mindedness, a French police force behaving as both the victimized and the complicit. They were an anti-Semitic terror squad and in their actions, the rule of law in France was inverted for the duration. Although French, this volunteer terror squad carried out the agenda of the Nazis.

By the time that Weil wrote her report, it was apparent that Stalingrad had been a turning point and from that moment onwards, the German war machine would be on the defensive. Further, the entry of Japan and the USA into the War had ensured that the military and industrial power of the USA would henceforth be fully available to the Allies in their struggle to liberate

Europe. The Free French in London recognized that they were in the best position, of all the political factions purporting to represent France, to take charge of the reconstruction of the country once liberation had been gained.

Liberating western Europe, however, threw up a number of problems for the Free French. There was the widely recognized moral affliction into which France had fallen. A return to the old dispensation was not desirable. The political travails of the Third Republic, with its constantly changing governments, its lack of continuity, its debilitating struggles between Left and Right and the extremes of the political actors within (be they Communists at one extreme or monarchists at the other) all pointed to the need to reinvent the French political system. (This was to result in the Fourth and then the Fifth Republics. The Fourth Republic, which lasted until the Algerian crisis destroyed it in 1958, was to revive France economically and to usher in the welfare state.)

Thinking French of all persuasions were distressed by the manner in which the moral fabric of France had been rent by the occupation. The dominant motive of those outside France resisting the Nazis, including those working for the Free French, was shame—shame at the rapidity of the French defeat and shame at French collaboration with the occupiers.

In this, her last work, Weil called for a return to a healthy patriotism after years of Communist internationalist propaganda, because patriotism was a close copy of community and social connection. She also called for it as an antidote to the moral corruption into which France had sunk. In Weil's mind, the State in France had killed off everything smaller than itself and true liberation of the human spirit in a postwar world for France would require a rethinking of the role of the State so that it did not simply continue to dominate and enslave people, this being, in her view, a high theme of French history. Weil's vision was that of global equality and brotherhood of humanity on the one hand and the need to form local and national politics (with this as its core ethos) on the other.

Central to any new political order, Weil believed, would be the place of work. Weil had consistently placed work at the center of social life and social organization. Consequently, a key to her conception of a renewed national mentality was to try to remove the alienation which modern work represented in the life of the worker or the farmer. If national culture was debased (which was the lesson of the German victory) if modern community was fractured, a major cause of this breakdown was the alienation at the core of work.

Related to this, Weil also promoted the idea of private property, which was necessary for the life of the soul, a means by which people could feel rooted in their environment and community. The early French socialist, Saint-Simon, had taught the slogan "property is theft" and this slogan became an institutional prejudice of the organized Left in France. Weil turned it on its head. The contemporary economic system, she believed, had to a large degree, divorced people from property in any personal sense, adding to their general alienation. People needed to possess property but the more that corporate structures intervened in direct ownership, through large companies with uninvolved shareholders or through agricultural collectives, the more alienated the individual worker became from the totality of community connections that should comprise life and make the soul secure.

More basically for Weil, however, for the soul to thrive, it needed to be rooted in the life of its community. She believed that the person needed to feel involved in the community, to feel he or she belonged and had a place in their community's geography and the history. Reflecting on the War, Weil concluded that one of the problems which it revealed was a widespread uprootedness, a tearing away of people from their community roots, a process which left them spiritually abandoned and existentially alone. Moreover, this uprootedness was self-perpetuating—uprooted communities caused other uprooted communities.

Weil also identified other causes of uprootedness in her analysis. These included money and education. Money acted as a cause because it gave a premium to the desire for gain at the expense of other people and came quickly to outweigh other motivations in the life of the individual. Education was a factor in uprootedness because, among other things, it had made culture a specialized pursuit divorced from people's national traditions. As well, technology and science had narrowed the culture of people and directed their attention away from anything which was not narrowly rational.

BACKGROUND: *THE NEED FOR ROOTS*

As we have seen, the most powerful evidence for Weil's belief in the pervasive uprootedness in France was the fall of France itself in 1940 characterized by inertia and alienation. Weil did not spare the working class in her analysis of recent French history. In the interwar years, the working class had been celebrated as heroes of society in the literature of countries on both sides of the Atlantic—authentic, suffering, real and bearing the hardships of their (factory) work with stoicism. However, she pointed to the fact that the working class, being uprooted, feared even more comprehensive uprootedness—that of unemployment. Weil acknowledged that modern work was mind-numbing and a shock to anyone who came to it for the first time. Part of this, she thought, would be overcome by what is now called the advance of technology, the invention of more efficient and productive machinery. The other part involved better education of the working class and their participation in intellectual life.

She did not subscribe to the view that culture could not be communicated to the working class because it was too high: rather, it was too low. It was a strange remedy, she said, to eviscerate high culture and dispense it in tiny doses. Culture, in her view, was about perfection and, in principle, everyone was capable of that.

For Weil the reason that education and participation were not attempted effectively was that the cultured class lacked the knowledge of how to translate sound culture to others in a language which they would comprehend.

On the practical means of achieving these objectives, which encompassed reinvigorating French communitarian roots including those of the working class, overcoming the deep alienation of factory work and contemporary farming and finding a language of cultural transformation which was effective, Weil's "practical" recommendations in her report proved less than fully practicable. She may not have realized the strength of scientific and technological change occurring in the world during and following the Great Depression. In any event, her practical recommendations demonstrated that Weil was referring to an industrial world already in the midst of profound changes. Moreover, politically, France and Europe were to emerge from the war into a world quite different from that which had existed at the start.

The period from the late forties to the early seventies were to see a continuous and steady expansion of the Western economies which enabled the widespread redistribution of income represented by the Welfare State. After the war, the problems of the prewar economies of Europe were relegated to economic history.

The world which emerged after the war, as if inevitably, saw a rapidly integrated Europe. This became a Europe which was eventually globalized, beginning with production and trade and taking advantage of the formation of the European Economic Community. The end result of this saw the migration of basic manufacturing out of Europe to what had been the economic periphery of the trading world. Europe itself, along with all high income regions, eventually saw the substantial disappearance of an industrial working class and its displacement by a hugely enlarged services sector supplemented and enabled by a continuing growth in international trade.

Weil's vision of the humanization of machinery to allow less stress and more training did in fact emerge, but not simply through better engineered machinery. It emerged by improved communications technology, growing computerization and vast leaps in the technology of automation which rendered whole trades redundant and demanded new modes of training and payment, all of which had the effect of re-skilling and de-unionizing the workforce.

Weil's analysis, as far as the practical application of her views went, likewise proved impracticable. However, one thing that remained of value in her writings on the culture of work and the needs of workers was her analysis of the need to fit the work assets to the capabilities of the worker rather than forcing workers into a regime of stress and fatigue dictated by the needs of the machine.

The value of *The Need for Roots* at the time she wrote it, did not lie in Weil's views on the future economics of a revitalized France, but in her ideas on the profession of politics, which, she said, needed to be reconceptualized if a new and worthwhile democratic world was to emerge. As Weil saw it, the reinvention of the French political system from the vantage point of 1943 implied the need for a set of national values to inform it and she set about identifying those values. The British had already undertaken a similar task and had produced the Beveridge Report of 1942. That report had identified the postwar tasks as tackling squalor, ignorance, want, idleness and disease but Weil went nowhere near those problems, confining her analysis to what she saw as the uprootedness that lay at their heart.

Politics properly conceived, in Weil's view, was an art and people needed to be educated in it as in any artistic striving. For her, education had to drive and enable perfection. What stood in the way of building a civilization of perfection was, first and foremost, a vision of greatness. One of the principal obstacles to the achievement of French greatness that Weil identified was the primacy of rights over obligations in the French (and by implication others') view of what should be normal in the political culture.

Despite the lack of practical applicability á la Beveridge, *The Need for Roots*, was written as a report on the future regeneration of France following the impending liberation. But Weil's theology was consistently interwoven through it, even if implicitly. What the Free French ended up with was a public policy report deriving from a theology. This could explain why it survived essentially as a work on the human spirit preparatory to the vocation of politics rather than as any practical expression of it.

The Need for Roots, when she submitted it, was not so much the report on regeneration which Weil was asked for, as a wide ranging excursus on the human condition, its spiritual malaise and the challenge of pointing people to the outer spiritual potentialities of their lives. It was an ambitious work in which Weil also attempted to draw out some practical implications of her spirituality for working life, and for the values that she believed should inform public policy.

In the end, *The Need for Roots* was not a work of public policy but a work of religio-political philosophy. That it proved of little use in putting together a blueprint for the regeneration of France was no surprise. For one thing, its focus was not on the practical side of public policy. But the best parts of it, what one might call the visionary parts, were very good and, had she lived and edited it, could have formed a new and vital contribution to the literature on human alienation and the spiritual emptiness that underlay it.

The Need for Roots is a challenge to read, partly because it is neither well structured nor polished. Additionally, much of it presupposed a future which did not eventuate. The real contribution of the work was in identifying the interplay of her spirituality and the working class struggle for life as it seemed to her.

ROOTEDNESS AND THE NEEDS OF THE SOUL

Her starting point in *The Need for Roots* was the question of the needs of the soul and to this end Weil began by asserting that obligations preexist rights. This latter was an arresting jumping off point for a French political report to take because France had carried the notion of human rights to the rest of Europe following the French Revolution in 1789. It saw itself therefore as preeminently the culture of people's rights. From Weil's perspective, the obligations which people had lay with the individual rather than any collective of individuals. This position would later lead her to discuss the role of trade unions and political parties.

Weil's initial concern in *The Need for Roots* was to locate obligation with the individual. Obligation was the quality which defined the person. The eternal obligation of the person sat side by side with his or her eternal destiny. These obligations linked to fundamental human needs, some of which were physical and some of which were spiritual. Such needs were basic to the shared experience which people had by virtue of their shared humanity. They were basic, too, to the functioning of the individual and to the collectives in which people found themselves.

The first human need that Weil identified was for order. She linked the need for order to the person's perception of the operation of the universe, an understanding of which, in turn, fed into the notion of wisdom and further to the capacity to pursue the good.

The second need Weil identified was liberty, the capacity to choose, and by implication the opposite of being a slave. She argued that rules that helped society flourish did not diminish true freedom as long as the source of their authority was respected. Moreover, for Weil, those who resisted benign authority would not be free under any form of society.

The third need was obedience, to rules and to leaders. In Weil's thinking, societies starved of obedience thereby opened themselves to those who would reduce them to slavery. Here she might have been reflecting on the history of the stormy years of the Third Republic.

Responsibility, the fourth human need, drew on Weil's memories of her brief periods of factory work. Responsibility was the capacity to make at least some decisions, or in special people, to lead others.

Equality among people was a further need by which Weil contended every person was entitled to the same amount of respect and consideration by virtue of being human. She concluded from this that a healthy society should demonstrate a vigorous ascent up the social ladder of those at the bottom and *vice versa*. Weil argued for equality of opportunity and economic betterment, both of which were constrained in the years leading up to the war but widely available in Europe after it. Weil's model of equality was based not on a theoretical view of people's position in the face of the law but on the origin and nature of the human person. Respect was due to all irrespective of accidental differences of status.[3]

In Weil's catalogue, respect for superiors or hierarchy appeared as a need because it was part of the symbolic universe which people inhabited. Her own role as a *professeur* in a profession (teaching) that demanded respect *ipso facto* probably informed this view, but really she was also arguing that people felt safer in a social system where superiors were respected and their judgment was trusted. Hierarchy, in *Roots*, was seen as necessary because it reduced alienation. Taken with the notion of access or equality of opportunity, hierarchy was a ladder up which people ascended throughout the course of their lives.

Honor was a further and related need and, properly considered, it also anchored the individual within society. One of the points Weil made was that people tended to honor those of passing fame and failed to honor the heroism of ordinary working people: indeed they generally failed to honor themselves.

Perhaps unexpectedly, Weil identified punishment as a human need. Her view of punishment, in a social context, was that it was a necessity for the human soul because it enabled reintegration in society. Punishment for crime placed the individual outside the social network and punishment could bring him or her back inside again. Punishment was an honor because it served to wipe out the stigma of the crime: having been punished, ex-convicts should therefore not suffer a permanent social stigma.

Weil saw freedom of opinion as a need of the soul. In discussing freedom of opinion, Weil reflected on the consequences of freedom of the press in France in the decades preceding the war. She argued the case based on her views of collectives (by which she meant any action of more than one person taken in concert), including professions and trade unions. Her ideal position was that writers of all types, including journalists, should be motivated by a commitment to the truth. As a statement of an ideal this was doubtless correct but decanting it into public policy raised obvious challenges. Weil advocated some version of press laws in the France that would follow the Liberation. It is a section where she appeared at her most intransigent, forcing the logic of truth as an ideal upon policy outcomes where the degree of disconnection with what was practicable was all too apparent.

Security as a further need of the soul was constituted by freedom from fear and terror. For Weil, one of the causes of insecurity, as far as the working class was concerned, was unemployment, a threat she observed in her periods of factory work when impending loss of a job could dominate the worker's life, consciousness and hence soul. The rise of the welfare state after the war, and France's extraordinary job security laws that were part of it, addressed this very concern. Although Weil had contended that every good action contained its own contradiction, she did not conceive of the debilitating effects of welfare on the individual soul nor the fact that Europe's job security laws would serve to lock out the younger generations of workers and condemn them to extended dependence on family, unemployment or migration. One question Weil did not consider was how security was possible for the whole of society, as distinct from selected minorities.

There is risk in all life, and Weil identified risk as a need of the soul irrespective of the degree of security. Risk, for her, was something of an outlet for courage. On private property, given that Weil was discussing roots and the needs of the person to be rooted in society and among fellow human beings, it was not surprising that she asserted that people needed to own a house and the accoutrements of their trade. Weil contrasted this with collective property and noted that the most common form of collective ownership was the factory. The factory, or the company that owned it, separated those most immediately involved in its functioning, the workers, from feeling a sense of satisfaction of their need for collective property. Weil was referring to the widespread alienation from work and its outputs that the modern market economy produced. Given her past sympathies with Marxism, Weil could be understood here to be making the case for both private and communal property ownership and noting that modern forms of property ownership satisfied neither of these needs. It would be interesting to see how Weil's analysis could have changed had she been able to foresee the eventual widespread deindustrialization of Europe and the ever-expanding role of the State that were to occur in the decades that followed.

For Weil, the most sacred need of the soul was Truth. She excoriated modern authors and journalists who went to no effort to verify the truth of what they said and were apparently indifferent to the manner in which their work affected others. Essentially, Weil argued for press censorship, an instance in which the logical ideal did not align with the actual possibilities of public policy.

CONNECTION AS THE BASIS OF CULTURE

These statements listed above about the basic needs of the soul lie in the introduction to *The Need for Roots* and could be seen as preliminary assertions. They had a strongly conservative tone and a dialectical style which served to expose the contradiction inherent in all human freedom. Robert Coles casts a helpful light on Weil's views here.

> Instead of apologizing for her, through a psychological or historical, or so-called contextual explanation of why she said what, one may as well recognize her stern reproving side, the streak of impatience that could turn into arbitrariness or self-righteousness. This went along with her strong devotion to certain moral principles: she detested the proudly amoral or value-free partisans of the liberal and radical intelligentsia. I think her social conservatism, her willingness to be punitive towards pornographers, towards various decadents, social and political, was an integral and persisting part of her, not some last minute aberration as her health failed.[4]

Having stated what she believed were the basic needs of the soul, Weil proceeded in the second part of her work to discuss the origins of the condition by which people became disconnected from their environment. Here she was on firmer ground.

Weil's view in *The Need for Roots* was that the uprooting of the individual was a common and perilous condition in any culture. The opposite, rootedness where it existed, was the network of bonds or bridges which subsisted among people giving them a sense of belonging and social incorporation. To paraphrase Weil, a person's most basic need within the society in which he or she dwelt was for roots which were bridges to others' roots. More prosaically, this was *inclusion,* which was an idea shared with others writing at the same time, especially psychologist Alfred Adler (1870–1937). The focus on the psychology of inclusion was a key theme in the social sciences in the interwar years, where a pervasive view developed that to understand the psychology of the individual one needed to understand the role and place of the individual in society. It was not surprising then that Weil, in looking at the alienation of the person, should have started with the person's social connectedness, his or her roots. These roots, taken collectively, might be said to constitute the total strength of a society and would determine its robustness in the face of evil. Weil reflected on this in considering the fate of France, whose sudden collapse at the beginning of the War demonstrated just how eroded the nation's moral strength was. France's fall, in her view was particularly galling given the modernity of the country, a modernity marked by the toxins endemic to any advanced country but particularly characteristic of France. These toxins were killing France's roots.

> The sudden collapse of France in June 1940 . . . simply showed to what extent the country was uprooted. A tree whose roots are almost entirely eaten away falls at the first blow. If France offered a spectacle more painful than that of any other European country, it is because modern civilization with all its toxins was in a more advanced stage there than elsewhere, with the exception

of Germany. (Uprootedness) was characterised in France by inertia and stupor... the country which behaved far and away the best was the one where tradition is strongest... England.[5]

Weil's reflection on the robustness of a culture raised the question of the relationship between past and present. An appreciation of the past of one's culture was a necessary adjunct to the connectedness she explored. She noted presciently, that the rootlessness of USA culture, given that it was an immigrant society, coupled with the fact that it was about to dominate the world, endangered the deep cultural connectedness of its people.[6] More to the point, she believed that we should try to remain connected to the past, partly because the future was unknown and partly because we needed to give to the future for that future to emerge. The past was integral to our understanding of who we were and it was the source of our collective self knowledge. She saw no necessary opposition between our notion of the past and our expectations of the future. The future, after all, did not yet exist and needed to be brought into existence but our actions in the present. To build the future which we desired, we would have to give it all that we could.

> But to be able to give, one has to possess; and we possess no other life... than the treasures stored up from the past and digested, assimilated and created afresh by us.[7]

The point of this discourse about the past was not for Weil to establish herself as some sort of reactionary. On the contrary, she was committed to the future but she could not see that the future which was emerging could be anything but alienating unless the best remnants of the past were enlivened and made effective. The passing of new laws in postwar France would be the easy part. The hard part would lie in seeing that working class demands pointed to something deeper, addressing the suffering engendered by alienation or a lack of roots. Weil saw working class calls for the nationalization of industries as code for job security. Opposition to private property she saw as code for wanting to feel part of a property owning culture, which people did not feel at the time and so on.

Much of Weil's thinking here was a plea for mutual concern and responsibility. She decried, for example, the fact that trade unions had no particular interest in the plight of unemployed working people who were not their members. She believed that they should hold just such an interest out of a common humanity and a common working class loyalty.

These underlying observations about the fundamental state of working people and their uprootedness from the rich culture of France, and by extension Europe, were profound. Weil's prescriptions for achieving this in postwar France, on the other hand, bore the mark of an unfamiliarity with economics and could explain why her report was ignored, as was, in the process, her underlying rationale and her plea for change.

THE SPIRITUALITY OF WORK

In Weil's views on the nature of work in the countryside (as distinct from the cities where the factories were located) were related to her observation that science and technology were expanding at a rate far in excess of people's spiritual growth. The countryside aped the city and rural life was no protection against the secularizing and alienating tendency for work to be despiritualized. There was a widening gap in both city and country between social and economic development on the one hand and spirituality on the other. Properly considered, however, Weil saw an underlying spirituality in work itself provided it could be recognized and cultivated. Talking about work having a spirituality would raise the general conception of the dignity of work and assist in reforming the enslaving tendency of modern factory work. She believed that even the Left could cope with the notion that there was a spirituality in work because the term was owned by no particular political tendency.

Even the Communists, in the present state of things, would probably not reject it.

> But one can only lay hold of such a conception in fear and trembling. How can we touch it without soiling it, turning it into a lie? Our age is so poisoned by lies that it converts everything it touches into a lie. And we are of our age.[8]

For Weil, the key to ending the uprootedness that characterized modern culture was to emphasize the spirituality of work. It would anchor the human person by giving a connectedness with the divine to the activities that loomed largest in people's lives—the work which engaged them.

Some variation of this line of thought existed in the world which emerged in Europe following the war because in the decades which followed, there was great effort put into making both factory and farm work safer through law and education. There was, as well, a slow increase in share ownership by ordinary people, which must have counted as something in reducing the alienation of worker from the corporation. Moreover, the general rise in the services sector saw a steady expansion in the number of self-employed people, small operators, that is, running their own businesses.

Closer connection between worker and product or output was one of the elements which Weil argued for. Most of the problems she observed in the countryside have since then been recast through the disappearance of the "peasant" and the emergence of the farmer, operating, in Europe at least, in a trade protected environment and shielded from the rigors of international competition. As in much of her work, Weil's policy prescriptions are now irrelevant because the world of production and work changed rapidly and in an unpredictable way after the war and with these changes the culture of work changed as well. What can be drawn from *The Need for Roots*, however, is the core idea Weil promoted of a spiritual dimension to that with which we occupy most of our waking hours—work.

THE STATE AND PATRIOTISM

Weil's treatment of uprootedness and the nation also stood on the assertion that patriotism should be based on compassion, not national grandeur. She contrasted patriotism with the internationalism which was the dominant ethic of Socialism in its many forms, including, Communism. For Weil, patriotism had to have an object and at its most fundamental level that object was people, the people who made up the total collective of the country, a collective which was only poorly represented by the notion of the State. Her concern, too, was especially to reinculcate patriotism into the culture of the working class, a patriotism long lost to them and reignited by the German occupation. The total moral collapse of France following the occupation demonstrated for her the piteous state of a people who could no longer feel trust or commitment to anything of substance. Even if the nation could regain its independence, the problem would arise in the future that France was no longer represented by the notion of community but only by the State.

> The State is a cold concern which cannot inspire love but itself kills, suppresses everything that might be loved; so one is forced to love it because there is nothing else.[9]

The lesson Weil drew from the emergence of the State in France, and by extension, everywhere else, was that the State killed competing forms of communal life and that it would itself survive every change of regime. The State machine in France, for instance, survived the abolition of the monarchy and lived on in the Republic and in every succeeding political dispensation. For Weil, the rise of the State, with its propensity to choke the life out of other forms of communal life in both city and countryside, was accompanied by the growth of a spiritual and intellectual wasteland. The Church, for example, by aligning itself with the monarchy (the State), cut itself off from the people, giving rise to the anti-clericalism which followed. Moreover, the rise of the State had been accompanied by a commensurate rise in the level of contempt for its operatives, like the tax authorities or the police. Public life in France did not, Weil said, arouse feelings of loyalty.

Weil extended this analysis to the sphere of religious faith. The State had separated itself from religion, making it a matter of personal choice. But this relegation to the personal ended up removing religious observance and the capacity to show public reverence entirely from the public sphere. Where religion was entirely a private matter it ceased to be a way in which the individual could begin to address the most important existential questions of his or her life, but became merely a matter of Sunday morning ritual. The notion that man's relationship to God was of small importance to the State Weil regarded as lamentable. Again, she believed, the State was thus projecting itself as the sole expression of community and the sole focus of loyalty.

> (Religion) is placed among the things which the State leaves to each one's own particular fancy, as being of small importance from the point of view of public affairs. Thus there exists nothing, apart from the State, to which loyalty can cling.[10]

Weil noted that Christians did not like having to make choices between God and country but the clear text of the New Testament demanded that they did. Christian life's first loyalty was to God, not the State. Christ, she pointed out, demanded that his disciples hate father, mother, brethren and so on if they chose to be a disciple of his. Weil pushed the reader, through her long and detailed analysis of the distant and recent history of France and the theme of the rise of the State, to a point where it had to be recognized that patriotism, for the believer, displaced God himself. It was impermissible to love one's country if that word "love" had a particular meaning. This was an especially surprising sentiment given the fact that Weil was at the time employed by the future government of France to draft a set of values for the nation. But, if one takes a step back and views her argument in light of the logic she posed, it was a statement of wide-ranging humanity. Patriotism, she concluded, given the reality of the world as it was, needed to be reimagined as a duty towards, a compassion for, people.

> It would be salutary for us to ponder the devil's terrible words with reference to the kingdoms of this world, as he showed them all to Christ. "All this power . . . is delivered unto me. . . ." Not a single kingdom is excepted.[11]

Again, Weil took Christ as her example. Christ showed not the slightest hint of patriotism in the accepted sense but he did weep over the coming fate of Jerusalem. His feeling was pity, not pride. Or, referring particularly to France, the great French patriot, Joan of Arc, did what she did because she felt pity for the Kingdom of France. Christians could love the State neither for its glory nor for its history, but only out of compassion for something precious that might be lost or destroyed. Compassion, she believed, was the appropriate Christian emotion when contemplating the nation because it alone was characterized by humility.[12]

By this stage of her argument, it was clear that Weil had moved well beyond the normal understanding of patriotism. Her overarching theme, however, was rootedness and her plea was for a patriotism that centered on people and the love one should have towards them in their affliction. Nations' destinies were contingent on the fortunes of history. Peoples' destinies, by contrast, were eternal and one's true *patria* was in the realm of God. Weil concluded by anchoring her plea for a renewed sense of authentic patriotism and grounding it in the then current existential travails of France but extending it to the entire universe. The pity that the French felt for France was the beginning of an opportunity to widen the general conception of compassion to embrace, not just France, but the whole of suffering humanity. France's sufferings were the sufferings of the world: France's lost and bereaved were the lost and bereaved of the world. The true nature of compassion allowed this.

> The very cold and hunger themselves then cause the love of France to enter into the body and penetrate to the depths of the soul. And this same compassion is able, without hindrance, to cross frontiers, extend itself over all countries in misfortune, over all countries without exception; for all people are subjected to the wretchedness of our human condition. . . . Compassion is, by its nature, universal.[13]

POLITICS AND FAITH

Weil died shortly after writing *The Need for Roots* a death hastened by the fact that she was attempting to live off the rations then available to the poorest in France. The sad circumstances of her death have been commented on by her biographers who are largely mystified by her apparent embrace of death in circumstances where she could have fought more determinedly for her life.[14] Her death does show, however, the determined and practical resolution of the compassion Weil felt for others and her resolution to live out in her own shrunken frame the cold and hunger that were her claims to patriotic love.

Weil's book, or report, shifted focus towards the end from an extended analysis of the human condition, the needs of the soul and the moral salvation of the nation, to a set of ways in which the nation or culture could grow roots again.

For Weil, people had to be encouraged to embrace the good and that necessarily involved for them a rediscovery of their spirituality. If a whole people were to be encouraged to rediscover its spiritual roots, then action needed to be taken by many actors, including the State. Weil here emphasized two phenomena, first the loss of religious faith among people and secondly the need to reinspire people with it if a more moral, connected and rooted society were to emerge.

Weil attributed the loss of religious faith and people's desertion of the churches to the apparent conflict between science and religion in the modern era. By science, she meant what one might call scientism, the view that empirical science constituted the most valuable part of human learning, to the exclusion of other knowledge. It was a view which took root in the cities but soon spread to the countryside because of the inferiority complex which rural people had with respect to those in the city. It had been particularly pernicious in the Soviet Union where the promotion of atheism had been state policy. Religion being the seedbed of faith, a rootless loss of faith soon followed.[15]

Weil considered that church-going continued among the middle class because it had some social cache. As the middle classes basically lacked religious faith anyway, the growth of the influence of science hardly affected their social habits, of which church-going was one.

For Weil, Christianity, with some exceptions, had become part of the structure of social exploitation because it was associated with those who benefited most from the social order as it existed. Her view was that the middle class might well need religion, but that need was not a legitimate expression of a relationship between God and man. The only legitimate basis for that relationship, as Weil saw it, was Truth. The reason one was a Christian was that it was true, and its truth was reflected in the fact that Christ claimed to be the Truth. This Truth did not impart to the individual a renewed energy for life (Christians were not necessarily vital people) but rather a renewed commitment to live out the Truth despite the consequences.

> Those beings who have, in spite of flesh and blood, spiritually crossed a boundary equivalent to death, receive on the farther side another life, which is not primarily life, (but) which is primarily truth; truth which has become living; as true as death and as living as life.[16]

The problem of religious people, as Weil saw it, was that those who had retained their faith became fervently attached to it, rather than to the Truth which should precede it. Given the primacy of Truth, however, the religious person should be prepared to abandon his or her religion altogether if it turned out not to be true, irrespective of the individual's dependence on it. Weil's view was that Truth, in this sense, was almost absent from contemporary religious life, as it was almost absent from secular life. This Truth was another name for reality and to desire reality was ultimately to love Truth. Weil's problem with science was that it had no commitment to the good nor was it against evil. Its only commitment was to facts.

It was here that Weil's analysis of science seemed to part company with the contemporary understanding of the nature of science. We generally hold that science operates on the principle of establishing a hypothesis and applying the logic of that hypothesis until we abandon it when a more firmly supported hypothesis comes along. For us, science advances by progressively displaced hypotheses, not by the compilation of an increasing aggregation of facts and behind a front of increasing certainty. A fact itself is an hypothesis. Scientists, or *savants* as Weil called them, may in fact have no commitment to the good in basic science as she said. But this is because they regard such a commitment as subjective and unhelpful. On the other hand, they may have a commitment to the good at least in the technology which flows from science, something Weil acknowledged.

Weil's views on science and truth led her to her true objective, the absence of real Truth, as she saw it, from religion. If science needed to start with a commitment to truth, so did religion.

For Weil, the first challenge to Christianity was to acknowledge the pervasiveness of holiness in the universe in its totality, rather than in the individual's heart. God's providence in this realm was, in the first instance, impersonal and was reflected in the laws of nature. One might petition God, but one needed to be persistent, largely to demonstrate to oneself that one was committed to the outcome one asked for and that one had with God a relationship of faith. God did not operate as a Roman emperor lording it over a mass of slaves and dispensing largesse to favored supplicants. This common perception was "absurd." The mysteries of Faith were absurd enough, but these dogmatic absurdities were "such as to illuminate the mind and cause it to produce in abundance truths which are clear."[17]

Imagining that God actively prevented harm to the individual or promoted welfare, a universal belief among Christians, was a very basic and pervasive blasphemy for Weil. It was, for her, a "ridiculous" idea to imagine that divine providence took the form of particular interventions in favor of individuals. For one thing, she held, it was contrary to our scientific understanding of the world, not to mention common sense.

> Unbelievers, not being inhibited by motives of reverence, detect easily enough the ridiculous aspect of this personal and particular form of Providence, and religious faith itself is, on account of it, made to seem ridiculous in their eyes.[18]

Or again, as she put it: "Divine Providence is itself the order of the world."[19]

What was actually sovereign in the world was what we could normally see with our own eyes; the fact that the world was ruled by limit, by contingency and by determinateness. This view and its repetition in her works points us back again and again to her foundational insights, namely that faith is a relationship with someone totally other, that there is a curtain between our life and that of God and that prayer is desire not petitioning God to change the already providential nature of reality.

In tying her discussion in *The Need for Roots* back to the nature of the divine relationship, Weil reached the end of her report to the Free French. It was a report that had wandered all over the terrain of human existence, starting with the needs of the human soul and making a case for re-anchoring the individual in a network of social roots as the first objective of public policy.

Public policy, as Weil saw it, needed to start, not with a socialist redistributive agenda, nor a free market celebration of the basic freedom of the person, but rather with the requirement for roots if the individual was even to start to have the needs of his or her soul met within the tangle of relationships that constituted community. Moreover, she tied these observations to the nature of God, a starting point that has confounded commentators ever since. Many commentators, admirers of Weil, have since attempted to deconstruct her insights. They have argued for them, and even for her practical policies (which are on less robust ground), while skirting the fact that she started her work with, and referred back continuously to, the idea that the world was a product of the will of God and that the duties we owed each other derived from the human nature we inherited, informed by our duties to God. In the end, Weil tied back human labor, (the source of all wealth) to death.

Death in Weil's view was, after all, the final limit placed on human endeavor. Death and human labor, two basic bedrocks of public policy, Weil connected in the end to God as well. Punishment should be celebrated because it allowed one who, through crime, had placed himself outside the collective good to be reintegrated into the community. So it was with man. Man had placed himself outside the realm of obedience to God. The punishment for this was labor and death. But consent to labor and death transferred the person back into the realm of the good and if man underwent these travails willingly it would represent an end act of obedience to the divine. In short: "Man's consent to (the) transformation (of death) represents his supreme act of total obedience."[20]

THE NEED FOR ROOTS IN RETROSPECT

Weil's long excursus into practical policy began with the needs of the soul for it to be rooted in the community in which it found itself. It ended with work and death which, in Weil's view, were to be celebrated because they reintegrated the soul with the goodness of God. Ostensibly a work preparatory to the political reconstruction of France, *The Need for Roots* was actually a call to duty and obligation over rights, to giving over receiving and to God over man. It placed work at the center of social life and proper social ordering, work that should be celebrated and respected as the heart of the striving of the nation. As for the nation for which it was written, there was, in Weil's view a higher calling to which a duty was owed, the totality of humanity.

It was small wonder that the report was deemed totally unsuited to the purpose for which it was commissioned. In a series of broad brushstrokes, Weil set public policy to one side and embarked on a kind of meta analysis of human interaction. She got to what she saw as the heart of the purpose of life, the real needs of the person, the reconstruction of social life, the obligations which the individual had to others, the primacy of work in human activity and finally, the place of man in a universe commanded by God where work and finally death were to be accepted and embraced as marks of obedience.

Where Weil actually did as she was asked, and drew out practical policies which needed to be implemented by a future government of France, they were illustrative at best. If one took her overarching philosophy from which these derived, however, the work could be seen as an analysis of the human condition that preceded any politics or any public policy prescription. There has been little else written in the history of public policy which includes such a comprehensive treatment of the nature of the human being and the place he or she has in the totality of the cosmos. That is why *The Need for Roots*, though hardly influential in the political sphere, has proven so inspirational elsewhere.

Weil's foray into public policy, which this, her last work, represents, proved to be a wider work of which the public policy aspects are the least important. Rather, it remains an explanation of rootlessness as the source of social alienation and force as the origin of rootlessness. Drawing on her past writings and especially on her reflections on the Iliad, Weil saw force as the element which objectified the person, turned the person into a thing. But in Weil's view, force need not be the final reality because beyond force was power, represented by the good, by love and truth and ultimately by God.

ON THE ABOLITION OF POLITICAL PARTIES

Finally, Weil had a related idea in *The Need for Roots* which fitted neatly with the exposition on the state of humankind contained in it. It was that politics could be carried on without recourse to political parties. It was an idea which was not original to Weil but she pushed it further than anyone else and tried to give it practical form.

It has long been generally believed that the role of the political party is crucial in the functioning of democracy. In most of the European parliaments, it has a somewhat different force than in the Westminster or Westminster-related parliaments, including those of the UK, the USA, Canada, Australia, New Zealand and India.

In the former, the voting system commonly directs votes first and foremost to a political party which nominates a listed set of candidates to attend the parliament and vote. The party is effectively the representative of a set of principles and policies which the voter chooses to support or which the voter declares best represents his or her political needs. It is a system which favors the promotion of issues and principles over personal one-to-one representation of an individual voter.

In the Westminster and related systems, the vote is for a person to represent the constituent on any and all issues. In fact, in most of these countries' constitutions, the party as such is not even mentioned. Parties exist, of course, but they emerge, as it were, after the event and are best seen as an artifact of the bargaining which ensues following the election with parliamentarians perfectly free to swap parties at will while continuing to represent the electorate which voted them in.

There are advantages in both systems. The besetting problem of the first system, favored in most European countries, is that it diminishes the responsiveness of the parliamentary representatives to the voter who put them there. The France of the Third Republic experimented with different systems with a significant degree of cynicism at play in an attempt by various political forces to gain permanent electoral advantage. But it was in looking over the border at other European countries that the manipulation of the democratic system by opportunistic, often short-lived, coalitions formed by unresponsive political groupings was most apparent. This was the origin of Weil's distrust of the political party. Given that she exempted the systems of Britain and the USA, we can assume that her problem was confined to Europe.

The problem Weil had with political parties as full and fair representatives of the people was that, as collectives, they necessarily acted to foment collective passion in the mind of members and among the general public upon whom they projected their views. Parties represented themselves primarily and were committed to their own survival and expansion. From being a means to an end (democratic representation) they became an end, focused on their own power and organic growth. The party everywhere, that is, had an inbuilt aspiration to power and control. The rise and expansion of the Nazi party in Germany through democratic structures was the chief and worst exemplar.

The positive element of Weil's approach to political parties was that she raised the possibility of democratic action without the intervention of the political party, a situation where representatives might exercise their own judgment and be held personally accountable for that judgment by the voters. The weakness in her radical proposal, as usual, was in the practical implementation which she proposed through press control and banning debate.

Weil saw this issue through the lens of French political history and especially the events of 1789 and following, when France experienced forms of democracy for the first time. The advent of the Jacobins in the National Assembly ushered in a long-term tendency for French (and by extension European) politics to be undermined by Jacobin tendencies.

The essence of the Jacobin tendency was the conception of the General Will, a notion that society's will could be captured, shorn of intervening irrational passion and represented in the Assembly by appropriate intermediaries. The evolution of this train of political thought over the period 1792–4 saw the progressive radicalization of the membership of the National Assembly, the expansion of Jacobin influence throughout France and the imposition of a reign of terror on those who disagreed with its views.

Jacobinism has been associated with the promotion of extreme left policies, an intolerance of alternative views, a distrust of power sharing and a will to utilize force, together with the punishment of political opponents. It has been a strong tendency in French politics ever since. The power struggles of the latter days of the Third Republic reprised some of these fears. They were exemplified in the attempt of the Left alliance conjured up by the National Front government to define and then impose its will in the difficult mid-thirties. Weil's own experience of democracy was soured by her parallel experience of political parties.

Weil's idea of banning political parties was beguiling but impractical. What her notion attempted to capture was the ideal of setting up a democratic structure where the representative was free to act according to conscience and with a view to the moral good of the constituency through the disinterested search for Truth. Given that, in Weil's view, parties corrupted the souls of their members by giving them camouflage for actions they would not consider doing unsupported, liberating them from parties would allow politicians to act morally. Any political collective, even of two, she believed, would begin to undermine both intelligence and morality. The party would colonize the moral purity of the individual and replace it with one or another variety of Jacobinism, and the triumph of force. If one wanted intelligence in politics, one would have to seek goodness first.

POLITICS AND THE COSMOS

What we derive from Weil's analysis of the existence of political parties is an insight into the deep-seated problems of any democratic system. An individual might consciously act in the interests of the Truth, but once two people were involved, this commitment would become diluted and by the time a party was formed, the interests of Truth would be totally replaced by a commitment to its own survival and growth. In the end, though people might be represented in a parliament, cynicism would inevitably replaced trust.

Weil's analysis of politics and the social order generally were linked to the purpose of the universe and the true nature of man. The universe, as she saw it, was holy, but man was not at home within it. To be reintegrated into this universe required the discipline of thinking through and realizing the truth. The person had to see throughout the contingent forces of society to the Power which lay beyond. People lived completely contingently in God's universe with a calling in life—to emulate the self-emptying of Christ in their own lives. Part of this was to minister to the affliction of others, to invite them to share the richness of human life and its best possibilities and in this to recreate the other person. That is what, to Weil, social responsibility really was.

Wrestling with Weil's vision today, including her vision of politics and the social order, necessarily involves us in both trying to understand her theology and in gaining an appreciation of its coherence. Her vision of life, relationships, love, Truth, politics, public action, patriotism and human suffering were all centered on the mystery of Christ, his self-emptying, his life, obedience, death and glorification.

In all this, Weil emphasized in her writings (and not just *The Need for Roots*) the central fact of human suffering, or at its extreme, affliction. It followed for her that the role of the State was to promote the good and to seek the Truth. In the political sphere, a divorce between faith and the State could not promote this. The sap of Christianity should be made to flow everywhere in the life of society.[21]

Despite its occasional unevenness, Weil's final work has long stretches of insight and anticipated much of the discourse which followed in the twentieth century concerning loneliness, alienation, the loss of community and the sense of purposelessness that pervades so much of life, both personal and political. As Coles said,

> She spotted the loss of familiarity, if not of family itself, which makes us so eager to invest a political figure with qualities that mitigate our loneliness and confusion and nourish our desperate striving for moral coherence. She spotted, too, how the self becomes our last refuge, the solipsistic withdrawal common to many who have material possessions and good social standing and whose indifference to politics . . . makes our lives all the more political: a "force" with which the various individuals who *do* care about politics will most certainly reckon.[22]

The world which Weil contemplated was a plane on which the competing forces of good and evil contended, but her viewpoint was not Manichaean and the evil she confronted in her work was not infinite. The world in which we found ourselves, she believed, was not the best that was possible because, while containing the whole range of the good, it also contained the whole range of evil. She believed that, historically speaking, the age in which she was writing was about as evil as could be. Beyond that, she noted in an enigmatic aside, evil became innocence.[23]

In Weil's view, the human being had an inbuilt longing for the good which was never satiated: this good for which people longed was ultimately God. That reality, God, was the source from which all that was good in people derived. Weil's contemplation of the divine, however, brought with it "absurd and insoluble contradictions." Nevertheless, every person had the power to turn to that reality: it was real insofar as it was exercised. It was exercised insofar as people consented to it.

Weil had two worlds, the realm of the person and the realm of God. She believed that people's longing for the good was really what connected us most immediately to God's realm. Everybody had that capacity whether they realized it or not and it was that shared capacity which bound us to each other. It was from that shared capacity to exercise obedience to God that the notion of our obligation to others derived. This shared reality opened people as well to the obligation of respect for others, an obligation to hold the other person sacred. Given the nature of the world, for Weil this link with the reality of God's world was the *only* basis of respect in a world marked first and foremost by an unequal distribution of power.

It was from that basis that Weil's political framework began. In looking at her politics today, one either accepts her starting point or does not. She was clearly speaking over the heads of her London peers as, generally speaking, political science focuses on the needs of the body both individually and collectively. Weil, as we have seen, started with the soul, with the needs of the body being a derivative from that.

The totality of the person with the complementary needs of body and soul gave the hint as to why the work Weil delivered into the hands of her superiors in 1943 was so wide of the mark. The political system which emerged one year after the end of the war ended up as a return to the party-based chaos of the Third Republic reinforced, in the Fourth Republic which followed, by the system of proportional representation which it adopted. True to form, the system labored on for years with frequent changes of government and a growing inability in the end to face up to the colonial question. It shattered under the weight of the Algerian crisis, a crisis which surfaced many of the contradictions identified earlier by Weil. Her work in this area still remains as a standard by which to judge the political system in any age, a standard which sees the person as embodied soul in a world where what really unites us is our shared access to the world of God.

NOTES

1. Weil, Simone. *The Need for Roots.* London and New York: Routledge Classics, 2002
2. ibid
3. Weil *Roots* p16
4. Coles, Robert. *Simone Weil: a modern pilgrimage.* Woodstock: SkyLight Paths Publishing, 2001 p 107
5. Weil *Roots* p49
6. Weil *Roots* p50
7. ibid
8. Weil *Roots* p97
9. Weil *Roots* p114
10. Weil *Roots* p126
11. Weil *Roots* p132
12. Weil *Roots* p170
13. Weil *Roots* p172
14. Coles *Pilgrimage* p18
15. Weil *Roots* p244
16. Weil *Roots* p246
17. Weil *Roots* p276
18. Weil *Roots* p279
19. ibid
20. Weil *Roots* p296
21. Weil, Simone *The Love of God and Affliction* in Panichas, George. *Simone Weil Reader.* Wakefield: Moyer Bell, 1977 p465
22. Coles *Pilgrimage* p74
23. Weil, Simone. *Gravity and Grace.* (Crawford E and von der Ruhr M *trans*) London: Routledge Classics, 1999 p21

Chapter Six

The Continuing Legacy

SIMONE WEIL:
HER ORIGINALITY AND HER LASTING SIGNIFICANCE

Weil published very little in her lifetime, certainly no books. Of the works which have been published since her death, none was intended by her to be published as a book and none was revised or edited by her. Perhaps this has been an advantage because we have access to her raw thoughts and feelings unmediated by any attempt to soften her ideas for a wider public. The unpolished nature of the corpus of her work nevertheless beguiles us and presents itself as startling and confronting. In examining what her lasting contribution has been, we need on the one hand to separate what was committed to paper as a result of her need to comment on the passing political and historical, from on the other, what was essential and permanent in her insight and in her writing.

As discussed in chapter 5, Weil's work on French reconstruction in *The Need for Roots* was uneven, with the more enduring sections being the parts not tied to specific public policies. In her earlier work on liberty and oppression, her reliance in the *Iliad* and her recourse to classical epic in general was novel but perhaps less than fully precise because of a tendency to read into the text the lesson she wished to draw out.

To find Weil's real and enduring contribution we need to take most seriously the themes which she took most seriously, her unsought possession by Christ when she was a secular agnostic Marxian activist, her transition to a lived experience of self-emptying and the internal dialogue which accompanied that. Weil's thought and her experience were united. Indeed, part of the overarching legacy which Weil left was an authentic unification of belief and action. Weil is still an arresting personality today because, although a thoroughly worldly woman, she lifted her perspective from the horizontal to the vertical at the very time when the intelligentsia of the western world were pronouncing on the death of God.

A number of markers emerge in an examination of her life and work. Weil was a non-religious Jew, but that seems to have had relatively little influence on her work, save that she explicitly rejected any Jewishness which others thought might partially constitute her formation in life. Of more consequence in Weil's intellectual formation seems to have been the (thoroughly excellent) bourgeois education she received, her immersion in the classics and philosophy, together with the strong commitment to the idea of France with which she was raised.

The fate of France ultimately became a pointer for Weil to the need for a more radical and inclusive universalism or humanism. Her periods working in factories and later in the field were brief and probably did no more than legitimize a set of views on the disempowerment of the working class which she already held.

For much of Weil's brief life she was an activist and propagandist of the Left and the truly important issues for the Left in interwar France included the capacity of the worker for revolution on the one hand and the possibilities of reform and improvement for workers in a capitalist economy on the other. Weil worked on these issues, as would be expected, but she eventually resolved the political issues through a theology of meaning, shifting her analysis from the plight and sufferings of people to the nature of the universe in which they existed, that is, the origin and purpose of one's life with its inevitable and necessary constraints.

Weil's starting point was the thrown nature of people's lives. Within the maelstrom people lived in, the individual could discern, if he or she wanted to, the pattern of the life of God and the nature of both the world which came into being through his will and the consequent relationship people could have with him.

For Weil, God's perfection and self-sufficiency dictated a world in which God had withdrawn to allow people to have their own existence. God, in her theology, lived outside the world and was utterly other than ourselves. People's cozy conceptions of a consoling God who duly answered their prayers in his personal providence towards them were illusion because the world could never be that way. God had already shown his providence in the laws of nature just as he had demonstrated the nature of his love in the life and death of Christ. The life of Christ represented in Weil the meeting in time of God with God, an extended act of obedience and complete trust in the absence of consolation. To know God, likewise, was to empty oneself of the personal, the ego, in a withdrawal to the impersonal and the perfect. To form a relationship with God was to pray and to pray was to attend or wait. The call to attend was meant, not just for God but for all whom people encountered; prayer was a universal attitude of reverence for the one addressed whoever that might be. This pattern of meaning and encounter were the basis of Weil's later writings and provided a pathway for her to describe and define all the major variables which she believed constituted the fulfillment of a person's purpose in life, to know God and to act authentically from that knowledge.

CONTEXT

Weil belonged to a particular place in the history of the twentieth century. The world was engaged in its midcentury struggle for survival and, improbably, she sought to place herself somewhere near its center, taking the small part she could and, eventually and in her own way, trying to assist with the coming reconstruction of Europe. In the last effulgent writings of her life, Weil sketched a series of approaches to what she saw as the central questions of humanity's existence—people's place in the world, the God who lay behind a veil of silence, the Void which defined people's lives and finding meaning in affliction within the Void, the pervasive grace of the universe and the mystical call to the annihilation of self.

Weil's moment in history passed. Evaluating her continuing contribution to the intellectual and spiritual life of today's world must involve, first, trying to place her writings in context and then seeing how much or how little of her insight actually depends on this context. Since Weil's writings began to be published after the War, she has been seized on and promoted by a number of writers as the standard bearer of a particular view or tendency. T.S. Eliot, for example, in his 1951 introduction to the English edition of *The Need for Roots*, believed that it was especially a book for the young before their minds and careers were committed.[1] On the other hand, Weil has been excoriated by many for failing to be what they wanted her to be, not socialist, not feminist, not religiously orthodox from some viewpoints.

Two things help in an analysis of Weil's continuing contribution. First, we need to separate out the last six difficult but productive years of her life and focus on this period, the productive terminus to which her life had led. Those are the years in which she wrote her best, most challenging and most coherent work and came close to as comprehensive a treatment of the lost human condition as anyone in the twentieth century has attempted. Secondly, we need to accept that she wrote from the perspective of a mystical theologian for whom everything ultimately flowed from a conception of God, indeed, an encounter with God if her own account is to be believed.

The central importance of encounter for her later writings makes contemporary dealings with Weil difficult for current commentators, although she is still quoted occasionally in articles by an assortment of writers. But to grapple with Weil in her totality means starting with her as mystical theologian and entering her own particular logic to find the pattern. The current default stance of most Western intellectuals, however, is secularism tending to atheism—a long way from mysticism. Coming from a stance which excludes God makes it more problematic today to perceive Weil's value to any ongoing discourse in politics or culture. Weil had no particular problem with atheism as such, but to try to make sense of her analysis of the human condition, love, truth, patriotism , politics, force or power, indeed any of the areas in which she wrestled, one must accept her basic discovery of God. This God, who had created or allowed the creation of the universe, left open an invitation to form relationship and encountered those who sought him, although leaving the person free to decide whether to continue the search, depending on what he or she made of the deep but divine silence at center of the encounter. To live in the contingent world, according to Weil, required a person to endure suffering and the appreciation of that suffering enlightened the person to the reality of the universe and the world. Weil's God was characterized by Truth and the manifestation of Truth in our world was Christ, the one who emptied himself of his divinity and then of his humanity and whose life provided the pattern for real faith. Annihilation of self was a prerequisite for real faith, as distinct from the shadow of faith which Weil thought was the form more often found in modern societies and churches.

The God Weil placed at the center of her theology sought out the soul from the vastness of his own existence. It was a God who encountered but then left the soul to struggle through the Void where the soul's outstretched finger might just touch the finger of God coming from the Void's farther side. Faith might follow. The core of Weil's faith was the path of the individual's own self-emptying together with total reliance on and trust in Christ who, in his final offering, transcended pride, self regard, ego and all that constituted self at the moment of his crucifixion and abandonment by the Father.

WEIL AND MEANING

The elaborate and moving metaphors with which Weil worked can be understood as a way of unpacking and explaining to a modern world the actions of God and the message of the New Testament. She has been criticized for her throwing over of the Old Testament but properly understood, she had a point. Old Testament theologians are generally of the view that it was as much pervaded by the notion of grace (understood as the opposite of Law) as the New. But the naive observer, which perhaps Weil was here, could be hard pressed to find such evidence. One needs to consider to whom she is speaking: a secular world on the one hand and, on the other, a church which purported to strive to pattern itself on Christ.

The original inclusion of the Old Testament in the Bible allowed the Christian Church to see itself as living within a framework of promise-fulfillment. Weil, however, did not begin with promise-fulfillment; her approach was indifferent to the view that the coming of Christ might have been anticipated and would represent the fulfillment of the Judaic journey. Rather, her theology started at the very center of Christian belief, the person of Christ, and repeatedly reflected on the meaning for Christ himself and for us of the working out of this singular life. As Weil's explanation deepened, so did the force and complexity of the metaphors she employed. Void, decreation, idolatry, cross, bridge, the Great Beast—all these and more were carefully explained but often via the agency of further analogs and slights shifts of meaning. We are, in her theology, clearly in the realm of argument by heightened language, even poetry.

To the extent that a *social* analysis falls out of this Christocentric view of the world and its history, it raises the problem that the poor and oppressed, who have had poverty thrust upon them, find themselves in the form of the image of Jesus, who took poverty upon himself. The most extreme deprivation, while annihilating the individual, can ultimately open the person to transcendence and grace. Weil's writing and thoughts are aimed at the individual in relationship with the divine. A social analysis would extend to groups of people acting as collectives. To some extent this is handled in *The Need for Roots*, but Weil is more a psychologist than a sociologist. As far as social analysis or politics go in Weil, collectives of people are inevitable but they undermine our personal responsibility to truth and our capacity for personal authenticity. This includes all political collectives and, incidentally, the Church.

A THEOLOGY OF THE EXTREME

Such are the parameters within which we must explore the work of Weil. Equally, they are the stumbling blocks which tend to confuse modern commentators on her work. To some extent, Weil represented a strain of Christianity which had existed within the Church for centuries, the participant-observer who reflected back to the community its own failings in both faith and obedience. She has been called heterodox because of the extremes to which she pushed the logic of her spirituality. Perhaps all heresy is just exaggeration, but when one pulls apart the line of thought in almost any of her theological insights—though she would have resisted the label theologian—one is still struck by the lucidity with which extreme assertion is pursued and defended. She may not have been orthodox, but she was logical. For example, on the non-presence of the Creator:

> God's creative love, which maintains us in existence, is not merely a superabundance of generosity; it is also renunciation and sacrifice. Not only the Passion, but the Creation itself, is a renunciation and sacrifice on the part of God. The Passion is simply its consummation. God already voids himself of his divinity by the Creation. He takes the form of a slave, submits to necessity, abases himself. His love maintains in existence, in a free and autonomous existence, beings other than himself, beings other than the good, mediocre beings. Through love, he abandons them to affliction and sin. For if he did not abandon them they would not exist. His presence would annul their existence as a flame kills a butterfly.[2]

This is certainly not the formulation one would find in any official statement of belief in the Church. But it upends and can extend our insight of an absent God. It is a way of contemplating the existence of God as giver, as active, motivated progenitor. Further, given that nearly all religious language is necessarily metaphorical, as Weil's was, one can only wrestle with the appropriateness of the metaphor she invoked. Again, on the ghastliness that so often constitutes human existence, she deftly integrates her central metaphor of the Void with grace, evil, truth and death. Enduring the Void is to choose to refrain from exercising power because the Void can be bypassed if one chooses. But it is grace that allows us to face and embrace the Void in ourselves. The energy to bring the Void into conscious existence has to be found within each of us. It is an energy which has to be found because it is the Void which demonstrates that we have a need for God. By definition, as it were, the Void contains evil because it lacks God, but the Void is part of the Truth each of us must face with all its attendant evil and lostness. Enduring this Void is the way of Truth, or authenticity, and leads to the obedient acceptance of death itself. Truth, as she points out, is on the side of death. It follows that any relationship with God has to be struggled for and involves a commitment to facing the reality of the Void within us if we are to reach Truth and an obedient acceptance of death. Her own life's journey, of course, followed this model.[3]

This model of the existential challenge of authentic existence is hardly a routine treatment of the theology of grace, but the metaphor of the Void does cast a different light on the notion of encounter with the divine. Weil's metaphors open up a world of mystery within the common everyday tenor of our lives, lived so predictably within the confines of our highly technological and, as she would say, scientific culture. To name the psychic terrain upon which we live as a Void to be embraced pulls the reader up short, especially the happy and life-contented reader. Weil shares with the more remarkable of the saints or theologians the capacity to draw the reader's attention to an alternative and mysterious reality. If we allow ourselves to deal in her metaphors we take in a view of life, our lives, from an oblique angle. Weil's words shock. So do the existential realities of her life with its illnesses, its frailty, its loneliness, its *malheur*. When these are put together we are presented with an alternative christological explanation of being where, on the one hand, the Void is the *necessary* context for encounter and, on the other, evil is one of the necessary accompaniments. *Her* Void is *the* Void. Weil the writer acted out in full view the implications of her utterance.

From today's vantage point, Weil's heterodoxy, often remarked on, is better regarded as a mode of expression, a way of arguing a point to the most extreme degree in order to elucidate the tension within the issue—*argumentum ad extremum*. Obviously, she differed in approach from the standard Catholic route but it was generally because she began with the notion of the individual as the basic datum of Christian encounter, not the church. It has been both a strength and a weakness of the Catholic view that practically all theology is begun within the intellectual confines of the church and is an exercise carried out for the church. The church, in the Catholic view, being founded by Christ, is the natural origin and end point of Christian dialogue about God, man and the universe. This view accounts for the fact that most Christian mystics have located themselves well within the structures of the church and have been duly recognized by the church, notwithstanding the variety of theological approaches they have proposed. Theology written from outside the confines of the church, however, has been predominantly a protestant endeavor: one thinks again of Kierkegaard, who mostly wrote theology as if the church did not exist, although he was formally Lutheran. Weil felt no need to write within any such ecclesiastical confines.

In *Gravity and Grace*, collected from among the spare notes she left with Thibon prior to her departure for the US, Weil sketched her view on the existential significance of God's action in the world. One must take these reflections as the basis of her thought, both before and after her departure from France. The accumulation of assertions, when taken together, form a kind of integrated picture even if the parts are varicolored shards. In *Gravity and Grace*, Weil sketched the reality of the existence within which the human being finds him or herself.

Weil's view was that the person, adrift in a world of suffering, would naturally seek solace and intervention from God but that the God being sought and worshipped in this suffering was quite probably *faux*. The God that really existed was quite different from the one we may have wanted. In *Gravity and Grace*, Weil puts before us a powerful image of God as compared with Louis XIV. The smile of the beneficent king is an imaginary reward, but is the equivalent of the investment that we have put into the relationship. The king's rewards have to be largely imaginary like this because his capital is limited. In a parallel way, we invent a God who smiles upon us but we want a more tangible reward and we believe we deserve it: indeed we have put ourselves in the position of God in an imaginary dialogue with ourselves, recognizing our desserts and promising to fulfill them. God, like Louis XIV, owes us. This notion of God as Sun King is deeply ingrained in popular religion, but not in the New Testament where we meet, as Weil points out, a God who emptied himself to the point of affliction, a self emptying renunciation that we are called to imitate. God as King, God as abandoned slave: as she would say, you can take your pick.[4]

For Weil, if one were to grapple with God, it might as well be the God who was real rather than the one of fond imaginings. This God came to those who accepted the Void of their own lives with no reward to counterbalance that Void. In her view, it was only the Void of the world that created the need for God.

So it is with our own lives and our own voids. The Void, if we follow Weil, is to be endured up to and including death but also creates the energy to receive grace. God has his own life, quite separate from ours but the separation is integral to the self-surrender of God in the divine *kenosis*. In Weil, God's life, though separate, is accessible and access to his grace is achieved through detachment from other things, an emptying of self. Affliction forces us to attach ourselves to things and this attachment represents our own lack of a sense of reality. Detachment from false reality is a kind of death because it involves a sacrifice of desire, a sacrifice of the personal in pursuit of the impersonal. God can be loved but cannot be possessed, even though, like the miser with his treasure, we do seek to possess him. Suffering, in Weil should lead to detachment. This detachment extends to everything, detachment from revenge, detachment from immortality, detachment from our comforting illusions about the nature of God. The miser is completely attached to his treasure buried in the ground. But this attachment to something hidden in the ground is a deprivation precisely because it is hidden. The God who is a metaphorical treasure in the ground in the same way is an illusion. He has withdrawn from us in order not to be loved like the miser's treasure. We must tell ourselves that this God we have concocted does not exist. We may reach a point of purifying atheism, thinking that God does not exist in any form. At that point, loving God in his impersonal aspect as we do, God will reveal his existence.[5]

Again from today's vantage point, Weil's analogies push us to the uttermost point of our own capacity to accept but they still serve to illuminate the powerful points she made. It is argument by analogy and the application of Occam's razor to the end degree. If we recognize this, we are in a better position to appreciate the depth of the affirmation she made. Here it is that suffering, with affliction its most extreme form, far from negating the reality of God in the world, actually establishes it.

The notion that the Good exists outside the boundaries of the world has been called transcendentalism. But Weil took it further. For her, the Good, which is Truth, could be *encountered*—indeed that was the point of the Incarnation of Christ. Moreover, she contended that our shared conscience knows what the good is that we strive to reach and, because we all share the same striving to the good, we all share in a set of deep obligations to other people. This in turn derives from a shared divine destiny and hence a shared humanity.

Taken together, Weil's later writings demonstrate a universal humanism where our shared humanity unites us by virtue of our shared destiny. But the individual can take only limited consolation from this universal humanism because, as is the general experience of humanity, the world we live in may be said to contain the Void which we must each choose to live through. It is a world where something big and vital is missing. One can quibble with the metaphor of the Void, but the reality of our own *lostness* in the world has long been a theme of both philosophy and sociology. Intuitively perhaps, we all feel to varying degrees that our souls live in a state of threat in the universe we inhabit, no matter what the force of our personality may be. Weil's is a powerful way of beginning to speak of God and his relationship to us. The Void provides a means by which we may, even if implicitly, define our lives. She directed us to embrace, rather than escape the Void and to do so by waiting or prayer. Again, Weil used a new language for an ancient insight. Detachment needs to be radical and the patient waiting that detachment leads to is satisfied. It is the only way of touching what is absolutely good. This radical detachment includes a detachment from the usual consolations of religion including that of the immortality of the soul because we are apt to confuse this with our current life and thus miss entirely the meaning of death and our radical need to accept, even embrace it. We need to detach ourselves from our folk notions of providence—we pray, God gives—because these notions do not pass the first test of common sense let alone the curtain of silence that necessarily separates us from God's life. Love, Weil holds, is nothing to do with consolation: it is light.[6]

In Weil's theology, the Void that characterizes our considered life is always being countered by our fertile imaginations which naturally seek to lead us from the Void rather than to embrace it. The gross weight within the Void is ultimately death and our imagination works to counterbalance the inevitability of death. But everything that counterbalances our death is a lie. Only grace, encountered within the Void is not a lie because it is not the product of our imagination. As Weil concluded in *The Need for Roots*, work and death are punishment but punishment is glorious because it reintegrates the individual into the world. The acceptance of the punishment of death, therefore, is a final act of obedience.

DEATH, SUFFERING, AND AFFLICTION

Death and its pervasive annihilation of all, as we have seen, were integral to Weil's thought. It was intrinsic to practically every issue she dealt with. Twinned with death, of course, came suffering and these two realities could not be escaped. Nor could the fact that these realities would always lead us to or away from God. Suffering was inevitable given the nature of the universe, but beyond that was affliction, an extremity akin to slavery in its effect on the soul which involved the loss of all, including any notion of the self and any connection to others. Weil dealt with the problem of evil (that is, how a God who is good could allow human suffering) in her analysis of the relationship between God and man. Suffering, which is the normal lot for the person, she believed, opened us up to the gap that must be crossed in knowing God. But affliction was an extremity well beyond suffering, a potential annihilation of the soul. Again:

> It is not surprising, either, that disease is the cause of long sufferings which paralyze life and make it into an image of death, since nature is at the mercy of the blind play of mechanical necessities. But it *is* surprising that God should have given affliction the power to seize the very souls of the innocent and to take possession of them. He who is branded by affliction will keep only half his soul.[7]

Affliction, in Weil, is the key to understanding the Cross, or perhaps the other way round. One enters into her view of affliction by considering it at a distance, rather as one contemplates the Cross. As Christ begged the Father for consolation and to be spared the ultimate in affliction at his crucifixion, that tearing apart of Father and Son was a statement of love, a mystery that linked abandonment with acceptance. The acceptance of affliction helped to explain the unity of Father and Son. The life and mission of Jesus were so bound up with both the goodness and truth which constituted God that they were ultimately an indistinguishable unity, a triumph across distance and separation

> The unity of God, wherein all plurality disappears, and the abandonment, wherein Christ believes he is left while never ceasing to love his Father perfectly, these are two forms expressing the divine virtue of the same Love, the Love that is God himself.[8]

Suffering, in Weil's theology, is not mysterious. Still less does it impinge on the reality of the love of God. Its necessity derives from the nature of created matter: the fact of suffering in a material world is as much an inexorable certainty as is beauty in a world created in love. But the lasting contribution Weil makes to our apprehension of the reality of the world we inhabit is that affliction, the most extreme suffering, the complete abandonment of the person in fear, pain and social exclusion, the fate of the slave, is also a moment in the life of God. It is the real consequence of the Incarnation.

Again in Weil's theology, the consolation of God is no sign of divine acceptance. Stripping oneself of all consolation creates the space for true faith devoid of illusion. Christ, who also lived through the absence of consolation, encountered the silence of God, the stumbling block in most people's search for God. God's silence is God's absence but the absence is the gap within which grace may be found. The absence of consolation in its most extreme form is to be found in affliction, the abandonment of the soul beyond suffering. Affliction focuses the soul on the infinite distance that separates the creature from God. In affliction, the creature, the person to whom this happens, is pure victim, pinned, as she points out, like a butterfly to an album. The person, though, abandoned, can continue to *want* to love because the most extreme suffering still leaves a consenting part of the soul free.

> He whose soul remains ever turned towards God though the nail pierces it, finds himself nailed to the very center of the universe. It is the true center; it is beyond space and time; it is God . . . this nail has pierced cleanly through all creation, through the thickness of the screen separating the soul from God.[9]

Weil wrestled with the problem of evil (which for her was really the problem of suffering) by an immense deepening of the problem: not just suffering but affliction. She resolved it by relating it to the meaning of the abandonment of Christ. One might or might not accept the christological explanation of human abandonment as offering insight into the balance of good and evil in the world, but insofar as an explanation of the meaning of the Cross goes, Weil's interpretation captures much of what traditional theology has consistently said, albeit in a manner which pushes the explanation further, linking the Incarnation with the central meaning of life.

SIMONE WEIL'S LEGACY IN POLITICS: CONTEXT

Weil wrote across a wide variety of subjects. She taught philosophy, was a classical scholar and attempted to be deeply involved in politics as represented in the struggles of the industrial working class. Occasionally, she synthesized her interests and wrote philosophically of politics or drew from classical epic to make a political point. Some of her earlier syntheses are still arresting in their argument, her work on liberty and oppression for example. Sometimes Weil's attempts to combine politics, philosophy and faith worked and sometimes they did not. *The Need for Roots*, Weil's final and somewhat uneven work, exposed her narrow political awareness. Perhaps the reason for the unevenness of the work was her own lack of exposure to democracy.

Writing in England, she addressed a set of French problems with the historic experience of France as her background.

French democracy is, and certainly was in Weil's time, a somewhat neglected child. In the English-speaking countries, the parliamentary institutions had evolved over long periods to represent local interests. Political representation grew hand in hand with the development of the free market economy and, indeed, even today markets and democracy are routinely seen as being inextricably connected. English politics were highly localized with most political decisions made at the local level and with central government decisions usually requiring a high degree of local consent. The political franchise grew slowly but the middle classes in Britain had strong representation in Parliament well before the middle of the nineteenth century. Following the lessons of the American Revolution, British colonial experience, was comparatively benign politically, with institutions of self-government established all over the British Empire when transplanted colonial populations sought them. To some extent, the USA experience followed the British with emphasis on a strictly limited role for government and a presumption in favor of individual liberty and government accountability. In all this, the underlying preference for democracy as the bedrock of government had been sustained.

The France in which Weil grew up presented a quite different political culture, a difference which she seems not to have fully understood. In modern times France has been a highly centralized country with, until the Revolution, a powerful monarchy exercising control over the most important elements of both the economy and the institutions of government. The advent of French democracy during the Revolution did not dim the preference of the French political class for centralized control. Nor did it seem to engender a natural commitment to free markets and the economic liberalism which normally accompanied democracy. Moreover, France's extremely powerful political tendencies lacked a developed capacity for compromise.

In the British system, when a political deadlock was reached, the administration would change, generally quite seamlessly. Occasionally, there would have to be a general election to realign the nation's political structures in a fundamental way. Likewise, in the USA, deadlocks could be handled by the powerful institutions of compromise established under the constitution.

In France, the first lesson learned by the Revolutionaries was that compromise was unnecessary if one could terrorize and kill the opponent. As a consequence, Jacobinism set up a revolutionary political tendency on the Left to use coercion and force to achieve political ends. The countervailing tendency on the extreme Right was a romantic nostalgia for France's past, exemplified by monarchism, clericalism and militarism. Between these extremes, reformers of various shades contended to form governments in a representative system where the capacity to respond to the local concerns of politics was generally overshadowed by notions of the national will, national glory, national destiny and national entitlement.

France's political mechanisms have, since the Revolution, been characterized in part by a pervasive cynicism of which Bonapartism, the urge to Empire and resort to the plebiscite have been emblematic. In Weil's time this complex of political forces was changing under the influence of communism and the French Left's partial embrace of it. Further complexity was added by the entrenched anarchist sympathies of France's strong union movement which, while on the Left, had split from the Communists in the latter part of the nineteenth century.

In Britain, at that time and by contrast, the dominant forces in politics were liberalism and conservatism, with some inroads being made by democratic socialism. Support for parliamentary democracy was so strong that it was rarely remarked on in political discourse. In the France of Weil's time, on the other hand, there were powerful and contending forces on both the Right and the Left, complicated by the bedrock cynicism mentioned above, and a widespread disenchantment with both the principle of democracy itself and with the Chamber of Deputies as its representative institution.

Much of Weil's despair about collectives in general and political collectives in particular seems to derive from her resigned observation of the French political system and her belief that central organs of government did not, because they could not, respond to the concerns of local communities or minority interests. This lacuna largely accounts for the sense one gets, when reading Weil on politics, that she is missing something, namely the influence of the national political culture on actual outcomes for people.

Weil's lasting legacy in politics, then, is restricted by her narrow political outlook. That, however, does not mean that she wrote little of lasting value here. Certainly, her analysis of power and force and their relationship was pathfinding. It is salutary to recollect, as she did in her analysis of the Iliad, that force nurtured delusion and eroded the natural human consciousness. Her views, developed in a number of works prior to the War, emphasized the point that force distorted the imagination of the collective, including, of course, the State.

Weil wrote extensively in a period dominated in Europe by Nazism, Fascism and Communism but the phenomenon of force, she pointed out, was as old as the Trojan War for which, at base, there was no motive save for the illusion of Helen. Weil's view was that in force, political discourse lost touch with the reality of experience. Force operated increasingly through the power of illusion and, having lost contact with the real, subverted language as it chipped away at limits, at pity and at order. People thought that they used force but ultimately force used them: such was the nature of war. The ardent revolutionary ultimately became a pawn of the blind mechanism of the unleashed revolution. The machine of force was no longer able to be stopped and ended up turning on its promoters for ends that were ultimately unintelligible to anyone.

So also, people imagined that they were free when in fact social force dominated and subverted them. That was perhaps why Weil wrote with an eye to pervasive social force when she defined in balanced pairs her list of human needs in *The Need for Roots*: order and liberty, obedience and responsibility, equality and hierarchy, honor and punishment, freedom of opinion and truth.

In Weil's thinking, if we were to recognize and name social force, we would need to start with a clean slate and define real and basic needs. In all this, language itself and people's care for its purity and truthfulness played a key role. Weil would have been highly sympathetic with her contemporary George Orwell's view, in *Nineteen Eighty-Four,* that language is an instrument of social force and can be deployed both to control and to define reality.

WEIL'S POLITICAL JOURNEY AND ITS LEGACY IN A TRANSFORMED WORLD

In asking the question of Weil's legacy and therefore her relevance to the twenty-first century we also need to explore some related questions about the times in which she lived as a contrast with the different times in which we now live.

Weil grew up and reached maturity in a period dominated politically in Europe by the struggle between Left and Right. This struggle was fought fiercely in the democracies as well as in those countries which succumbed to totalitarianism of one type or another. More particularly, Weil grew up in the France of the Third Republic which was beset with particular problems and particular fears. Following the First World War, as Weil was approaching adolescence, France was a victorious Allied power, having defeated Germany and rebuilt her economy. It was an easy environment in which to reflect on the attractions of pacifism. The rejection of all forms of military preparedness was a worldwide phenomenon.

Weil's early rejection of all forms of national rearmament can be understood as typical of the times. The basis for these pacifist ideas never really left her and one of her enduring strengths has been that, intellectually, little was finally discarded: ideas were reintegrated and redirected to more robust conclusions.

Weil never changed her views on force and the insidious hold which it had over the human imagination, even after she had changed her views on war and struggle. France in the interwar years, however, was enduring a period of long term weakness. It had a low birth rate, and in that period, security was strongly affected by demographics. It had an economy marked by low investment and slow growth with little real connection to the ideals of democracy.

When Weil was twenty-four, the Nazis took over in Germany. The world was amazed at Germany's subsequent transformation as the Nazi Party seemed to revivify the country by expanding the economy, providing greater employment and unleashing a wave of powerful patriotism. Following the German government's reoccupation of the Rhineland and its Anschluss with Austria, it was apparent that none of the Allies was prepared to enforce the Treaty of Versailles and to limit Germany's reckless aggression. France prepared for war again but even then was not able to transcend its entrenched political hatreds sufficiently to meet the enemy with any sense of moral determination or military aptitude.

All these factors went into the formation of Weil's views on politics, suffering and ultimately the transcendent importance of the individual in a world adrift in a vortex of force.

Clearly, the fall and humiliation of France was a catalyst for Weil's final writings on the human being in relation to politics. France laid low did not, in her view, rise to the occasion. It was apparent to every commentator that the German occupation exposed, not the best in the French character, but the worst. Even now, the story has not been fully written of the moral pit into which the French sank in the period 1940–1945. Collaboration with the Nazis, the active pursuit of Jewish French citizens to hand over to the occupiers, the continuing war conducted by the colonies against the Allies and the daily betrayals (both big and small) carried out at all levels of French society: all these and more are of a piece with the exposure Weil saw of the underlying moral vacuum that France had become.

The emotion Weil felt was shame and in her last writings, she sought to separate the individual from the generality and to expose the corrupting influence that all collectives necessarily had on the soul. In this way Weil thought the collective might be made less toxic and the individual might learn to interact with the collective in a more informed and ethical manner.

Weil's concern with force, power and aggression was paralleled with her concern for the industrial and rural worker. Although her attempts to identify with these workers through her brief stints in factory and farm work were unsustainable, due to her poor health and her professional career as a high school philosophy teacher, Weil learned enough about factory conditions to write coherently on the alienation of work and the radically unrevolutionary mentality of the overburdened worker. Again, these observations and lessons were not wasted and were to inform aspects of her work repeatedly.

The world which emerged after the Second World War, two years after Weil's death, and for which she thought she was writing, faced a set of realities quite different from what she had imagined. The Left Right divide continued but it slowly narrowed as the contradictions of Communist ideology were exposed. Within the democracies, the progress of the welfare state cut the ground from beneath far Left coercive policies. Militant Left activism became confined in most countries to the outer reaches of the trade union movement. Factory work became more benign as increasing complexity demanded greater investment in worker skills and capital. As well, the resulting increase in productivity gave scope for higher earnings. A fifty year process of expanding world trading opportunities through a variety of global institutions followed. This meant that the benefits of trade began to flow to everyone through cheaper goods and higher standards of living. France and Germany began a process of integration, still continuing, to eliminate the chances of any future conflict.

Fifty years after her death, the social and political drivers which impelled much of the Weil's work were blunted or simply disappeared. Who now worries about international Communism, German militarism, worker control, poor factory conditions, colonial exploitation and trade unions? Some of these issues attract attention from time to time but the dominant issues of the age have moved well beyond them. Indeed, Europe itself, the basic starting point of Weil's consciousness and analysis is no longer the cultural center of the world.

THE PERSON: THE CALL TO THE IMPERSONAL

In Weil's construction of personhood, it was what she called the impersonal which was sacred. It was the impersonal which put all people on an equal footing in the sight of God. This was why she pointed out that the greatest achievements of humanity were never noticed, because their heroes were nobodies, people hidden away and achieving great deeds in lost and lonely places, like factory workers or miners. The geniuses of the world, on the other hand, were the beneficiaries of random luck, such randomness being an unavoidable facet of the universe we lived in.

God himself had an impersonal aspect, which was the embodiment of truth and a life quite separate from that of the person. It was this radical separateness that was the basis of both the Void and the curtain of silence which masked God.

Weil wrote that everybody had a sacred impersonal life. The fact of the impersonal existence of the soul meant that people could live their lives imbued with love and committed to truth while believing themselves to be atheists. For her, this atheism was misnamed because those who lived in and sought to love were already in communion with God in his impersonal aspect. These seeming atheists, for want of a better category, included those who had pure love of neighbor and were capable of accepting the reality of the world, a reality which included affliction. Love of people and endurance together defined those who loved God in his impersonal aspect. They might think of themselves as atheist but they were not: they were wholly converted already to God in his impersonal aspect.

Where does the providence of God come in? Providence, normally understood as the intervention of God in the affairs of the world, his answering of petitions or even guiding history, had little place in Weil's writing where there operated an entirely different notion of providence, one in which the natural laws of the universe were evidence of the providence of God. One would have had to be blind or heartless to believe otherwise, that God intervened for one person but not the other, or even that God intervened at all. God's non-intervention was precisely an outcome of his perfect impersonal nature.

Where God became personal Weil held, we experienced the cry from the cross, "My God, my God, why have you forsaken me?" This was the cry of everyone nailed to the cross. It was the cry of God to God. God's non-intervention was itself an aspect of providence because the order of the universe was fixed, created in love and the outcome of wisdom. It contained evil because that was inevitable. There was no "problem" of evil (how a good God can allow evil to happen to good people) because the world could not be otherwise. *Allowing* evil to happen was the obverse side of allowing the creation of the world and evil's existence therefore also could not be otherwise.

People, as Weil said, had a personal and an impersonal aspect. Our self was what emerged at birth and this was impersonal. Our social or personal self, by contrast, was formed over time, a growing carapace which imprisoned, as it were, the real or impersonal self. The impersonal in Weil was formed through grace while the personal in us was will. Self-emptying *(kenosis)*, which was at the heart of her theology involved a deconstruction of our social selves and an immersing of our selves in the *im*personal aspect of our own personhood—a journey from will to grace. In Weil's thinking, we should not compare ourselves with others if all we were doing was comparing personalities or ego. True humility lay in comparing ourselves negatively with the *im*personal lives of others. What was emptied in the journey of grace would be social conditioning and it was this conditioning which we must escape. Personal love was emotion: impersonal love was attitude.

In Weil, there was a curtain between the person as creature and God. This distance also served to illuminate the problem of evil in that God's necessary distance from us pointed to the depth of his own self-abasement in the Incarnation, his love being proportional to this great distance. The cross was the sign of this: God in the midst of what is cursed and otherwise distant from God.

Affliction could be redemptive (just as joy could be, incidentally) because, since suffering was nothing but blind necessity, to accede to it constituted obedience to the divine. The love of God, therefore, had two modes, joy and suffering: one was gentle, the other a wound. Both were aspects of the relationship and the mode, joy or suffering, did not matter provided we understood the experience. Moreover, the fact of suffering could only be experienced through the veil of the silence of God.

THEOLOGIAN OF THE TWENTY-FIRST CENTURY

To consider Weil's continuing legacy we must really weigh the nature of her theology, and the manner in which that theology speaks to the present age with its different realities. This is in essence what has truly survived as a deposit of lasting value.

The point has been made that Weil's theology and the spirituality that derived from it were non-ecclesial. They were defined outside the confines of the Church. To a large extent it is this which still gives them their freshness. Dogma hardly figures in Weil's theology except as a way of meditating on the truth which might underlie its expression. Nor do the structures of the Church carry weight. They are part of the "collective" against which the individual must struggle to avoid losing his or her soul. Even prayer, which one might think the Church would have some sort of monopoly in describing, is unique in Weil's writing. It is constituted, as we have seen, by attendance or waiting, but that attendance may be centered on the encountered human being as well as the Other: they are elements of the same phenomenon. The Church, Weil believed, had a tendency to put itself between the individual and Christ, as if the Church owned Christ. But of course it does not and the transparency and directness with which Weil described her unsought encounter with Christ reminds us even today that, though the Church might be the community by which the narrative of Christ is continued from age to age, it does not own the subject of story.

Coming to this story as she did from outside the confines of the Church, Weil saw things with fresh eyes. For Weil, atheism, as has been said, far from being a denial of God, maybe an implicit affirmation if one accepts her personal/impersonal description of both God and us.

Weil reinterpreted, ever so slightly, the idea of grace, a biblical idea developed over two thousand years within the Christian community. The grace of God, she believed, pervades the universe and reflects an aspect of God himself. The providence of God is not seen in the dispensing of largesse from heaven. As she said, one would have to be heartless to believe this. Providence in Weil's view is there as an attribute of creation, as the laws of nature, in fact.

Weil's interest was not in how to get on the good side of God but rather how to allow a relationship with the Other, who is necessarily silent, to come into being in the first place. Once there is this relationship with God, the silent and effectively departed Other, people's attendance, their prayer, should be directed at stripping the self of the personal and becoming impersonal and without ego.

How do we know this? As Weil observed, we know this by examining the relationship of Christ in affliction with the Father. Stripped of all claims to humanity, Christ remained obedient and loving to a silent and absent Father. Christ was the one without ego, the one who obediently took death upon himself and loved in the absence of love. Christ and the Father are ultimately God and God.

This is a long way, as Weil would say, from deciding how to spend an hour or two on a Sunday morning. Given her own experience, Weil clearly saw that the intervention of the Church might or might not be helpful in bringing the individual to Christ, especially as the initiative rested with the other side. Most members of the Church, as a collective, Weil believed, were too in love with religion and too little in love with Truth. But it was only Truth that mattered because it was only Truth which could reveal the true nature of the world and the true nature of people's lives.

In Weil's own case, she was "possessed" by Christ and the subsequent experience of trying to empty herself of all attachment drew her closer to Christ while making her less and less capable of affirming, perhaps less tolerant of, ecclesial structures. Weil's commitment to Truth was almost absolute. One cannot imagine her, for example, echoing the sentiment of another mystic, St Ignatius of Loyola, who, in the interests of thinking with the Church, urged members to hold that black was white and white black if the hierarchy of the Church so defined it.[10] That was the inverse of Weil's thinking and she abhorred any departure from complete commitment to Truth in the interests of accommodation with mere collectives. For Weil such surrender could only put the soul in danger.

The idea that Christ can be found outside the Church is a modern one but Weil lived that experience without the slightest fear of contradiction in a way which is instructive, especially in the world which emerged after her death.

From today's vantage point, and noting that Weil was largely outside the Church, we also need to grapple with the fact that she was a mystical theologian in the tradition of those who have been the subject of unsought, unmerited possession by Christ.

There is debate about whether Weil's "possession" by Christ actually determined her work, in which case she might have had a mystical experience without being a mystical theologian. She was, after all, an extreme individualist and it is possible that she compartmentalized her mystical experience from her theological reflections. One can equally take the view, as here, that Weil's theology was presented in such a cast that she wrote with a confidence born of personal and unique insight, in which case the description of mystical theologian is acceptable.

In trying to appreciate this aspect of Weil, one encounters one of the greatest stumbling blocks to a modern understanding of her. We, today, do not expect intelligent and sophisticated thinkers to claim to have been appropriated by God. Most especially, we do not expect someone who once described herself as an atheist and who was known in adulthood as a Left wing firebrand and Marxian philosopher to make this claim. Modern commentators, including feminists, stumble on this point and writers have tended to step around it. Accepting Weil's claim is a difficult thing for many to do but her own self-understanding, especially in the last six years of her life, was absolutely centered on the dynamic memory of an encounter with God and a revelation of Truth which informed all her subsequent writing—all those writings that are, in fact, of permanent value.

Weil's encounter with the divine cannot be understood as some end-of-life aberration in a life otherwise devoted to an incisive humanism. It is essential to understand her encounter, and indeed to accept it, if we are to place Weil in her proper place as a writer and activist. That proper place is something like philosopher-theologian-mystic and each element is germane to the assessment of her lasting contribution.

The twenty-first century offers a markedly different terrain for the evaluation of Weil's work than did the century for which she wrote. As all political writings eventually become, it is clear that her political writings are of historical interest only. The attraction for today of her theological writings, on the other hand, lies partly in the fact that they do not presume attachment to any "collective," certainly not to the Church.

The comfortable bourgeois views on all questions relating to theology and meaning which prevailed for the first half of the twentieth century have, since the Second World War, been eroded. But Weil's work relied on none of these views. For example, she had no place for natural theology. In her view the only indication we can have, this side of the curtain, that there is something on the other side, is not the beauty of the world and the fact of man, but suffering. Moreover, what is on the other side, as it were, is not a Roman emperor inverting or raising his thumb to various intercessions, the folk view of intercession, but a silent God the knowledge of whom is subjective and self-authenticating. In Weil's theological approach, we know God not because we look at the world and discern him, but because he has sought us at the same time as we have sought him.

Alternatively, we know God existentially, even if we believe we are atheist, because of the love exhibited as part of our *im*personal makeup. To those who seek God, as Weil said, God will reveal himself and we shall know that revelation when it comes irrespective of the subjective shape in which it comes.

Religion, in Weil's view, is of little help. We can only hope that it does not stand in the way. What is life-authenticating is not adherence to religion but the discovery of faith. In reflecting on why Weil's theology and spirituality should hold an attraction for the twenty-first century we might start with her radical individualism. This is an alluring quality for our age in which every facet of our culture, driven by a pervasive technology, conduces towards conformity of views and the suppression of the individual's unique capacity to discover the impersonal self in relation to others and to love others with complete altruism. Total altruism eliminates the personal self, as it did in Christ, the self-emptying one. In finding this, we find that faith introduces us to a new mode of being, one based on Truth, not illusion. Faith, in other words, is a possibility of Truth open to every person.

Faith, in Weil, is also another word for recognizing reality, the reality of the curtain of silence that necessarily masks God and the reality of our own existence delimited by suffering and ultimately death (both ineluctable products of the gift of life). Finding our own soul in the midst of this reality means finding the means to discern the truth that is the underlying reality of the universe. We do this by eliminating self and thereby leaving the space to open ourselves to God. Faith, in other words, conduces to the relationship of prayer.

We have seen, too, how Weil navigated the problem of evil, the stumbling block which people encounter first in contemplating the action of the divine. Gustave Thibon summarized her approach to the problem of evil as the challenge to escape the gravity which is within ourselves. Although God comes to us through the "thickness" of time and space, his grace does not affect the continuing operation of the blind and random forces which operate in the universe, and have to operate because they are elemental forces of physics. The difference which grace does make is to wait for us until, in silence, we turn to God and wait upon him. The gravity within us is a natural concomitant of creation whereas grace acts to assist our decreation, our ability to endure the reality of the world in all its stark threat. In this we must not succumb to our imagination which only serves to keep grace out.[11]

The problem of evil is the problem of existence and the response needed is to endure the blind necessity of the world in which we find ourselves. It is, however, the biggest stumbling block for those who ask themselves about the possible nature of God. Weil's response was stark and unyielding: there is no problem because it could not have been otherwise.

We must finally ask ourselves the question about the changed nature of the world in which we find ourselves today and especially whether people are still in any sense reflective. Do people, indeed can people, still reflect on the most fundamental question, that of *meaning* within the universe in which they find themselves. It is the real question to which Weil addressed herself and for which she provided a framework for responding to it. The world we have inherited is radically different from the world of 1943 but Weil's works contain insight into a future world for which in many respects she equipped herself and potentially us to address.

One of the dominant forces which have swamped western culture and, to a large extent, non-western culture as well, has been secularization. In western countries, this process of de-sacralization has been encouraged by the progress of science and technology. It has also grown under the influence of urbanization whereby people in small rural communities migrate to large urban centers lacking the cultural supports to religion. As social life becomes more complex, it also tends to encourage a mental differentiation in the lives of individuals. There is a tendency, that is, for areas of life, like religion, to become consciously distinct and less and less a function of community participation. The secular sphere in modern life is especially the world of work and is dominated by the State and the economy. This world of the State and the economy has become increasingly differentiated from and dominant over the sphere of religion. As Weil observed, the role of religious participation has declined to a minimum under the influence of such pervasive secularization.

Technology as a determining force in culture is a subject that has been taken up by a number of modern writers, but very eloquently by the Canadian philosopher George Grant.[12] Grant believes that the sacred in life has been consumed by the relentless progress of technology and that our former widely shared perception of the vertical plane which links us to God has been replaced by a completely horizontal plane in which we cannot see beyond the world view which modern technology has delivered to us. Technology's unhindered progress through the world and the illusion it creates of human self-sufficiency have constructed a world where Christianity and its apprehension of the supernatural are doomed. Society is less and less the outcome of considered interactions built on an appreciation of the shared fatherhood of God, than the unplanned outcome of an army of self-aggrandizing human beings promoting their own individual interest. Human freedom has morphed into an all-consuming technological will to power which pushes society forward on the horizontal plane towards a totally secularized future without any identifiable end or purpose and without ethics except those temporary and contingent laws created by individuals themselves.

This dynamic force, in Grant's view, has a cost. It destroys the environment because it has no regard for the sacred in creation and it destroys man by eliminating any consciousness of the eternal from human life. In effect, anything is permitted because God does not exist. For Grant, Christianity cannot accommodate itself to this technological nightmare. It cannot be of this world and at the same time not of this world. To the extent that it accommodates itself to this situation it negates its own supernatural values.

To a large extent, Weil would have accepted this view, although she named the malign force science rather than technology.

It seems largely true that the structures through which we now live our lives, including the collective structures, are already secular and by and large the sacred is relegated to a collection of artifacts of history. This phenomenon is compounded by the way in which we are becoming, in many different facets of our lives, a less historically aware culture. We are less and less conscious of the process of history of which each of us is a product. History is poorly taught at school, if at all. The notion that it has relevance to our self-understanding has slowly been eroded as both school and higher education curricula are crowded out by the subjects thought to be more necessary for survival and prosperity in the technologically dominated world in which we live. Universities have little commitment to the disinterested search for truth for which history would be an essential element. Rather, they are now universally transformed into job training centers disconnected from any higher purpose. The media, too, has seen a decline in the art of journalism and, with that, a widespread decline in the consciousness of political and cultural history, that is, history as people in the past would have remembered living it.

This loss of history make the framework of Christian narrative fragile because it is, after all, a religion based on a particular view of history—promise followed by fulfillment. For a generation which does not understand history, myth can fade into fairy story. Moreover, the churches cannot make much difference in this because they have faded from view as faith has eroded and they too have generally succumbed to the almost irresistible force of economic growth and the technological explosion which has driven it.

It is to this highly technological world, where people have forgotten who they are or what they exist for that Weil still has the capacity to speak. In her own time, Weil saw the extreme difficulty involved in attaching faith to the structures of religion. She supported church structures and the encouragement of religion by the state because they were part of the culture through which a predisposition to self-reflection and religious self-questioning were made possible. Weil's emphasis, however, was on the individual, the singular person who actually seeks to encounter the Other and to endure the silence and doubt which necessarily go with that. These individuals still exist as they do in every age.

Weil shared with Kierkegaard the idea that there were too many Christians, that the veracity of Christianity was to be found in the individual—the thinking and grappling soul who struggled for in a world where others had effectively given up. This individual could justify a whole generation. The example she offered was the cow: the entire creature produced the milk although it was only drawn from the udder: such was the way of saintliness in our world.[13]

Apart from that, of course, the default atheist may, in his or her impersonal aspect already be close to God and to be living a life that already reflects grace and understanding.

There are other aspects to Weil's life and views which have as much relevance today as ever, perhaps more so. Her theology leads to a sense of realism about the facts of our existence, especially that suffering and death are part of the meaning of life and that they do not negate the reality of a God who must be perceived through silence. Weil's theology leads us to a humanism of personal self-effacement where attention to the other person, the person in need, has the effect of prayer. Finding God does not require religious structures and it does not require church, though these may facilitate the journey. Weil simply reexamines and restates the insight of the Gospel of John, that those who seek will find. Hers is not really religionless Christianity nor even anonymous Christianity. It is rather a theology of universal openness to anyone who wants to deepen his or her understanding of the relationship of God to the created world. The path to this is ultimately an emptying of self.

Taken together, Weil's spirituality is one encompassing the silence of God, the tenuousness of our grip on understanding "the problem" of God, the fact of suffering and its necessity, the acceptance of death as obedience, the model of Christ as absolute self-emptying, the cross as bridge to God, prayer as attention or waiting and the providence of God as nature's laws. All these seem as much a robust set of building blocks for a spirituality for the twenty-first century as is now possible.

We cannot put the genie of secularism back into the bottle: any spirituality for our age has to overcome the cognitive dissonance we often have between faith, however conceived, and the known complex variables of our lives. These include the chance creation of the universe, the struggle to discern purpose in the universe, the lived contingency of ethics, the difficulty of affirming any sort of natural theology or natural law and the persistence of meaningless violence and, as Weil would have termed it, force. They also include the impoverished and outdated language in which a watered down faith is offered by the church in our time. These variables generally stand in the way of faith today.

Weil's stark spirituality provides a response to these stumbling blocks, one which is adult and unapologetic. To the extent that faith is sought in our unfolding century, her insight provides a way into it completely devoid of illusion and completely affirming of the otherness of God. No illusions and no false comfort: that will be the final gift of the spirituality of Simone Weil.

SIMONE WEIL AND THE CATHOLIC CHURCH: HER FINAL CONTRIBUTION?

In Chapter One it was remarked that Weil was possibly a saint. In fact, the Roman Church would not have the imagination to canonize one so challenging and, in her own way, so thoroughly Catholic. But Weil's final and best contribution may yet be to challenge and assist in the reform of the Church.

The Church has not been in a healthy state for many decades. The Eastern churches, for example in Russia, are still hankering for the force of the state to protect them and have little sense of mission. The main Protestant churches have been in crisis for a hundred years and their total secularization is well progressed. The Catholic Church, organizationally strong until the end of the 1960s in the West, has been enduring a long period of organizational erosion and more recently an unimaginable set of sexual scandals which has largely destroyed its once formidable moral authority. Each successful action it does take to serve the world today tends to turn it ineluctably into just another non-government organization. An aging laity lack passion and the clergy seem to have settled for survival.

Weil's spirituality, however, holds the church to a standard which ultimately cannot be evaded. In the first place, the Church's faith must begin with the individual soul in encounter with Christ. Waiting on God and devoting one's attention fully upon him cannot be evaded as the essence of prayer. Secondly, the collective of the Church, though of divine origin, is in constant danger of reducing the challenge of faith, as all collectives must, rather than heightening it. This heightening of faith can only be achieved by lowering the individual and the collective ego—a retreat, that is, from the personal to the impersonal where perfection is to be found. Thirdly, to the extent that the soul finds God comfortable, or comforting or responsive to special petitioning, it is worshipping a false God. The reality of God in Weil is to be found in the cognate realities of suffering and death. It is only the God or, more specifically the Christ, that we find in these interstices that can be real. The Church needs to challenge itself to refrain from offering false comfort and to turn people's minds to the meaning of the inescapable realities of suffering and death. Faith ultimately has little to do with dogma but everything to do with the retreat from the personal, an individual *kenosis* where the personal self retreats to create room for God, encountered in heightened attendance, an attendance of no different quality in principle than care of neighbor.

A Catholic Church that is more catholic, that is inclusive of a wider variety of people and backgrounds, that takes a commitment to Truth more seriously than an obsession with sin and which does not worship itself, all these are elements of the transformation that Weil proffers.

Whether the Catholic Church will survive in any but a vestigial form is an open question. One thing is beyond doubt. The world does not need more non-government organizations. What it needs is truth, and the community of the church is one of the few ways in which the ingress of truth into the world can be assisted. The gift that the Church can offer the world is to point to this Truth. Words and witness are the essence of what it has to offer in this endeavor. Weil, an example of sublime integration of words and witness, is the exemplar of both.

> It does not rest with the soul to believe in the reality of God if God does not reveal this reality. At a time like the present, incredulity may be equivalent to the dark night of St. John of the Cross if the unbeliever loves God, if he is like the child who does not know where there is bread anywhere, but who cries out because he is hungry. [Forms of the Implicit Love of God] [14]

NOTES

1. Weil, Simone. *The Need for Roots.* London and New York: Routledge Classics, 2002 pxiv
2. Weil, Simone *Some Reflections on the Love of God* in Springstead, Eric O. *Simone Weil Essential Writings.* New York: Orbis, 1998 p79
3. Weil, Simone. *Gravity and Grace.* (Crawford E and von der Ruhr M *trans*) London: Routledge Classics, 1999 p10
4. Weil *Gravity* p9
5. Weil *Gravity* p15
6. Weil *Gravity* p13
7. Weil, Simone. *Waiting for God.* (Crawford E *trans.*) New York: Harper Perennial, 2009 p69
8. Weil *Waiting* p74
9. Weil *Waiting* p81
10. Puhl, Louis SJ. *The Spiritual Exercises of St. Ignatius.* Chicago: Loyola Press, 1952 p160
11. Weil *Gravity* pxxii
12. Grant, George. *Technology and Empire: Perspectives on North America.* Toronto: House of Anansi, 1969
13. Weil *Gravity* p144
14. Panichas, George. *Simone Weil Reader.* Wakefield: Moyer Bell, 1977 p488

Bibliography

A NOTE ON SOURCES

There is a lively academic discourse on the life and significance of the work of Simone Weil as there has been since her work began to be published after the War. This is no less the case for works translated into English than for those published in French. Unfortunately, the vast body of academic work available in English has failed to make Weil's work commensurately accessible to the introductory reader. Many interested and intelligent people find much of her work, if unassisted, almost impenetrable. This is probably because very little of her later work was written with a view to publication. Moreover, much of what has been published should probably be regarded as first draft—work which Weil might have refined had she lived longer.

    I have tried to make this volume easy to follow for the introductory reader. I have, as a consequence, tried to ensure that the works cited are few and both easily available and fully accessible. The select bibliography which follows, therefore, points the reader to works which are well known in Weil circles, are readily available in libraries and which enable the reader to extend his or her level of understanding of Weil's work in easily grasped stages.

    All but three of the works cited are in English. All are basic and I have tried to keep to a small corpus of works so as to assist the introductory reader who may have ready access only to these introductory works. The three works in French are for those with the interest to try them in the original.

    For readers interested in the life and work of Sören Kierkegaard, I have cited the introductory biography by Walter Lowrie and his last journals (edited by Ronald Gregor Smith). For those wishing to pursue the spirituality of

Ignatius of Loyola, who has been referred to in this volume, I recommend the Spiritual Exercises as translated by Louis Puhl S.J.

SELECT BIBLIOGRAPHY

Coles, Robert. *Simone Weil: a modern pilgrimage.* Woodstock: SkyLight Paths Publishing, 2001.
Grant, George. *Technology and Empire: Perspectives on North America.* Toronto: House of Anansi, 1969.
Kierkegaard, Sören. *The Last Years - Journals 1853-55.* London: Collins, 1968.
Lowrie, Walter. *A Short Life of Kierkegaard.* Princeton: Princeton University Press, 1974.
Miles, Sian (ed). *Simone Weil an Anthology.* London: Penguin Classics, 2005.
Panichas, George. *Simone Weil Reader.* Wakefield: Moyer Bell, 1977.
Puhl, Louis SJ. *The Spiritual Exercises of St. Ignatius.* Chicago: Loyola Press, 1952.
Springstead, Eric O. *Simone Weil Essential Writings.* New York: Orbis, 1998.
Weil, Simone. *Attente de Dieu.* Paris: Fayard, 1966.
Weil, Simone. *Gateway to God.* (David Raper ed.) Glasgow: Collins, 1974.
Weil, Simone. *Gravity and Grace.* (Crawford E and von der Ruhr M *trans*) London: Routledge Classics, 1999.
Weil, Simone. *La Pesanteur et la Grâce.* Paris: Pocket, 1991.
Weil, Simone. *L'enracinement.* Paris :Gallimard, 1949.
Weil, Simone. *Oppression and Liberty.* Abingdon and New York: Routledge Classics, 2001.
Weil, Simone. *The Need for Roots.* London and New York: Routledge Classics, 2002.
Weil, Simone. *Waiting for God.* (Crawford E *trans*.) New York: Harper Perennial, 2009.
Weil, Simone and Rachel Bespalloff. *War and the Iliad.* New York: New York Review of Books, 2005.
Wills, Arthur (trans). *The Notebooks of Simone Weil.* London: Routledge and Keegan Paul 1956.

Index

Abolition of political parties, 87
Affliction, 25, 26, 43, 56, 59, 102; as redemptive, 109; heart of Weil's theology, 90
Anarcho-syndicalism, 15
Assisi, 5
Atheism, 46
Authenticity, 4; challenge of, 98; existentialism and, 51

Barth, Karl, 6, 47, 62
Beveridge Report, 74
Biblical criticism, 45

Catholic Church, 47, 117; dogma and, 47; indolent, 61
Christ suffering and affliction, 26, 34, 42, 58
Collective, 105; hostility to, 30
Communism, 17, 46, 105
Consolation, 5, 28, 103
Culture, 77, 79

Death, 63; and annihilation, 102
Decreation, 37; faith as, 41; central to Weil's theology, 41

Encounter, 49
Europe post war, 73
Evil, 58, 103, 113; problem of, 64

Faith, 35, 46, 50; and prayer, 53; loss of, 84
Fascism, 1
Force, 39
Franco Prussian War, 11
Free French, 71
French democracy, 104

God, 25; abandonment of man, 98; compared with Louis XIV, 99; encounter with, 41, 95; human longing for, 91; impersonal nature of, 54; knowledge of, 40; love of, 37; providence of, 34; silence of, 4, 38, 116
Grace, 43, 110
Grant, George, 114–115
Great Depression, 14
Gravity and Grace, 23, 35

Health, 15
Holiness, 85
Humanism, 101

Iliad, 25, 26, 93
Impersonal, 108
Incarnation, 36

Jacobins, 89, 104

Kenosis, 34, 36, 37, 52, 99, 115
Kierkegaard, Soren, 29, 30; and angst, 51, 52; and existence, 50; death, 50; debt

to, 36

Modernist movement, 48
Mystic, 53; as stumbling block, 66
Mystical theology, 49, 55

Natural theology, 46
Nazism, 1, 17, 46, 105
New Testament, 82, 96
Need for Roots, 3, 4, 7, 15, 21–22, 23, 24, 69–91
Needs, 75; equality, 75; freedom of opinion, 76; hierarchy, 76; honor, 76; liberty, 75; obedience, 75; order, 75; punishment, 76; responsibility, 75; risk, 77; security, 77; truth, 77

Obligation, 75
Old Testament, 46, 96; Promise and fulfilment, 97
Orwell, George, 2

Pacifism, 13
Paris, 8, 11
Patriotism, 65, 71; and Christ, 82; and the State, 81
Perrin, J-M, 6, 20, 47, 64
Philosophy, 3
Political legacy, 103
Politics, 39; and faith, 83
Popular Front, 16

Portugal, 16
Prayer, 28; attention as, 40
Providence, 85, 109
Public policy, 86

Self emptying. *See* kenosis
Science, 84
Second World War, 18
Solesmes, 18, 28
Spain, 2
Spanish civil war, 3, 16
Spirituality, 49, 60
Spirituality of work, 80
Spiritual legacy, 60
State, 81
St. Ignatius Loyola, 5, 6

Technology, 114
Thibon, Gustav, 14, 20
Third Republic, 12, 89, 91
Towards the Proletarian Revolution, 16, 55
Treaty of Versailles, 12

Vichy, 20, 70
Void, 43, 95, 96, 100, 101; As psychic terrain, 98

Waiting for God, 18
Westminster system, 87
Weil, Andre, 2, 11

www.ingramcontent.com/pod-product-compliance
Lightning Source LLC
Chambersburg PA
CBHW070644300426
44111CB00013B/2249